AMERICA LOVES®
CHICKEN

AMERICA LOVES® CHICKEN

101 All-Time Best Recipes

LINDA WEST ECKHARDT

Illustrated by Mona Mark

WINGS BOOKS

New York • Avenel, New Jersey

This 1993 version is published by Wings Books,
distributed by Outlet Book Company, Inc., a Random House Company,
40 Engelhard Avenue, Avenel, New Jersey 07001,
by arrangement with GuildAmerica Books®/Doubleday Book & Music
Clubs, Inc.

GuildAmerica Books® and America Loves® are registered trademarks
of Doubleday Book & Music Clubs, Inc.

AMERICA LOVES® CHICKEN was prepared and produced by
Michael Friedman Publishing Group, Inc.

Random House
New York • Toronto • London • Sydney • Auckland

Printed and bound in the United States of America

Library of Congress Cataloging-in-Publication Data

Eckhardt, Linda West, 1939-
      America loves chicken / Linda West Eckardt; illustrated by Mona
Mark.
          p.   cm.
      Reprint. Originally published: Doubleday Book & Music Clubs.
      Includes index.
      ISBN 0-517-09377-4
      l. Cookery (Chicken) I. Title.
TX750.5.C45E34 1993
641.6'65--dc20   93-8669
                                                        CIP

8 7 6 5 4 3 2 1

For Mildred Marmur

ACKNOWLEDGMENTS

I wish to acknowledge the cooperation and support offered by the National Broiler Council, who taught me plenty about chicken and showed me just how versatile this food is. In particular, I wish to thank Dot Tringali and Ralph Gregory of Newman, Saylor and Gregory, as well as George B. Watts, President, National Broiler Council.

CONTENTS

Introduction

The wine chills. The chicken roasts; once it's done, I'll braise some lettuce and carrot shards. I'll pop open a jar of pickled baby beets. The glistening golden bird will sit in its own nest of braised lettuce with carrots, and bright red baby beets will peek out from under the breast. My guests will think I've cooked all day. In truth, the entire preparation time was less than fifteen minutes, and that included setting the table.

The humble chicken has been a constant companion at the dinner table since 2000 B.C., when man first began trapping wild red chickens in the jungles of India.

Then, chickens were considered sacred and appear in artistic representations of the period on pedestals, to be consulted for omens.

Later, after we began eating chicken, priests still offered up the less edible parts to the gods. Entrails were sometimes cut open to assess man's fortune.

Sometime around 1350 B.C. the chicken had worked its way west, as evidenced by the chickens found painted on the walls of Tutankhamen's tomb in Egypt. We know that by 720 B.C., chickens had made it to the European continent, because some sleepyheads had them barred from an Italian town that year for crowing too early in the morning.

The modern-day chicken frequently comes to market already boned and skinned, making chicken the homemade convenience food for the 90s.

Chicken is naturally low in fat and cholesterol, yet full of nutrients and delicious. Pound for pound, it's one of the best bargains at the meat counter. I did a comparison study in my home-test kitchen and came up with surprising results on the economy of whole chickens versus parts. First, I boiled a whole chicken. By the time I skinned and boned the bird, I had discarded nearly half the weight and was left with about 9 3-ounce servings. I then cooked and measured chicken

how sold	gross weight	unit price & cost	edible meat	# servings	per-serving cost
whole bird	4 lbs. 15 oz.	@.79 = 3.28	26.7 oz.	9 servings	@$.36
thigh-legs w/bone/skin	16.1 oz.	@1.69 = 1.96	9.5 oz.	3 servings	@$.65
4 boneless thighs, skinned	9.7 oz.	@2.29 = 1.39	9.7 oz.	3 servings	@$.46
1 whole chicken breast (2 halves) w/bone/skin	16.7 oz.	@1.69 = 1.85	9.8 oz.	3 servings	@$.62
2 chicken breast halves boned/ skinless	8.6 oz.	@3.99 = 2.14	8.6 oz.	2 servings	@$1.07

parts, both boned and skinned and boneless, skinless. The actual cost per serving is shown in the chart above.

When you factor in the time it took to skin and bone that whole bird, the already-prepared pieces began to look like the bargain, particularly the boned thigh meat which was cheaper per serving in my market on that day than the bone-in pieces and only costs a dime more per serving than a whole bird.

In this book you'll find a lot of recipes for chicken breasts. Since there's confusion about a half breast and a whole breast, what this book means by breast is a *half* breast, boned and skinned, that uncooked weighs about 4 ounces. Remember, that breast will shrink to 3 ounces when cooked. A good number of recipes call for thighs or thigh-leg combinations. These parts are interchangeable in recipes and can be substituted at will. You can also substitute boneless thigh for breast if you prefer its deep rich flavor. Also included are recipes for whole birds. There is nothing quite like a whole roast chicken cooked with fresh herbs.

The chickens used to test these recipes were all "grocery store broiler-fryers". In cases where a roasting chicken, or other type—such as game chicken or Cornish hen—could be used to good advantage, it is noted.

I came to these particular recipes by several routes. I considered the changes in chicken marketing, the fact that more pieces are sold today than whole birds. I thought about our growing sophistication regarding ethnic foods. I thought about how little time we all have. And last, but not least, I thought about health.

The recipes were selected based on these changing trends. According to a Gallup Poll conducted in the spring of 1991, Americans like chicken prepared in Italian, Mexican, Spanish, and Chinese and other oriental dishes. One of the most interesting changes emerging from this melting pot we live in is that cooks are beginning to fuse these old world cuisines. Japanese-French and Caribbean-Mexican are two examples of so-called "fusion" cooking. This trend is well represented in the recipes included herein.

To find out what America's cooking these days, I first went to the 1991 National Chicken Cooking Contest. Some of the best recipes from the 1991 contest are included here. It was clear to me that America's eating more chicken, that we want it cooked quickly and/or easily, and that we want to cut down on fats and cholesterol.

To that end, we've updated some American classics by reducing fat and cholesterol in the preparation. Oven-Fried Honey Pecan Chicken for example (see page 115), which is actually roasted not fried, bears little resemblance to the fat-cholesterol load you get from deep-fried chicken.

In fact, thirty-seven recipes included here have fewer than 300 calories per serving. If you're trying to diet, you'll find chicken preparations can be high in satisfaction, yet low in calories, fat, and cholesterol.

Because time is so valuable today, the recipes included have been selected based on the ease of preparation, as well as good taste. Whether a dish is quickly

A FEW WORDS ABOUT SAFETY

• Choose chicken with fresh, pearl-colored flesh. Don't buy chicken with dark bruised places, and watch for the expiration date. Buy the freshest chicken available.

• Refrigerate chicken immediately upon returning from the market. Use it within a day or two, or freeze it.

• Thaw frozen poultry in the refrigerator or microwave set on "defrost", never on the counter.

• Use hot soapy water to wash your hands, utensils, cutting boards, plates, or any other surfaces touched by raw poultry.

• Don't leave raw poultry at room temperature for more than thirty minutes.

• Although chefs prefer to cook poultry to an internal temperature of 160°F, the USDA recommends cooking it to a temperature of 180°F. This may make the meat seem dry to you, but it's the safest temperature, and that's what is recommended in this book.

• Cool cooked poultry rapidly and refrigerate immediately.

• If you plan to marinate poultry, make twice the amount of the marinade, refrigerate half of it in a jar, and marinate the bird in the other half. Discard the marinade in which you soaked the bird, then baste the cooking bird with the marinade you saved in the jar.

• When cooking poultry in the microwave, always cover tightly with plastic wrap so that the steam created kills any bacteria. Take care that the plastic does not touch the food. Rotate the dish once or twice to insure that the chicken has cooked evenly, then let it stand a few minutes before unwrapping.

• To reheat cooked chicken, place it in a microwaveable serving dish, cover and microwave on 100 percent (full) power for 2 minutes per serving. Or heat in a 350°F oven about 10 minutes per serving.

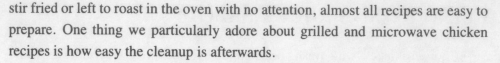

stir fried or left to roast in the oven with no attention, almost all recipes are easy to prepare. One thing we particularly adore about grilled and microwave chicken recipes is how easy the cleanup is afterwards.

You'll be glad to know that you can skin a chicken *after* it's cooked and eliminate more than half the grams of fat per serving. According to a study reported in the September 13, 1990 issue of *New England Journal of Medicine,* an oven-roasted chicken breast cooked and served with the skin has 193 calories and 7.62 grams of fat. Skin it before cooking and it has only 142 calories and 3.07 grams of fat. Remove the skin after cooking and you get exactly the same nutritional results, 142 calories and 3.07 grams of fat per serving.

Just remember, to decrease your intake of fat, skin poultry before you eat it. Chicken fat doesn't migrate beneath the skin on a chicken, but it will find a home on your hips if you eat it.

The nutrition data included in this book presumes a cooked 3-ounce serving and originates with tables provided by the United States Department of Agriculture (USDA). If you weigh food in your kitchen, remember that uncooked chicken weighs more than the finished product. Part of cooking is boiling away some of the water in the food.

Many recipes say "salt to taste." Please note that I salt food minimally. If you load your chicken preparation with salt or soy sauce, the sodium content of the dish you prepare can rise dramatically.

Gladly, we can say that at the end of this project we liked chicken better than when we began. We've learned a lot of new methods of preparation, and have updated some classics.

Chapter 1

APPETIZERS, SALADS, AND SOUPS

Tex-Mex Chicken Zip Fajitas
Chicken Avocado Flautas
Chicken Potato Empanadas
Buffalo Chicken Wings
Sautéed Oysters and Chicken Livers
Saltimbocca
Chicken Liver Turnovers
Chunky Chicken Sandwich
Cranberry Chicken Salad
Tom Parker's Sort-of-Chinese
Chicken Salad
Chicken Stock from Scraps
Thai Coconut-Chicken Soup

Tex-Mex Chicken Zip Fajitas

Pop these zippy chicken fingers into a hot flour tortilla with additional salsa and your choice from refritos, grated cheddar, and finely chopped lettuce and tomatoes for fajitas that are better than any you can buy.

serves 4
1 hour

½   **cup reduced calorie mayonnaise**
¼   **cup fresh salsa**
1   **teaspoon chili powder**
4   **(4 ounce) skinless, boneless chicken breasts**

1. Preheat charcoal or gas grill.
2. Combine mayonnaise, salsa, and chili powder in a bowl. Add tortillas and chicken breasts, cover, and marinate about 20 minutes while the charcoal fire heats.
3. Grill chicken over very hot fire, brushing with marinade. Grill until fork tender and done, about 4-5 minutes. Cut cooked chicken into strips.
4. To serve, hold a hot flour tortilla in your hand, spread with hot refritos, chicken strips, cheese, sour cream, salad, and salsa.

Per Serving: 287 calories; 38 g. protein; 46 g. carbohydrate; 13 g. fat; 126 mg. sodium; 114 mg. cholesterol.

To make an impromptu salsa, choose two very ripe tomatoes, then combine in the food processor with ½ onion, 1 jalapeño pepper, a handful of fresh cilantro, and salt and pepper to taste. Pulse to coarsely chop. Adjust seasonings, cover, and refrigerate.

To make an instant guacamole from this mixture, simply mash a couple of avocados, add a spoonful of this salsa, and stir.

Per Serving: 270 calories; 31 g. protein; 23 g. carbohydrate; 15 g. fat; 230 mg. sodium.

Chicken Avocado Flautas

Flauta means "flute" in Spanish. These meat and vegetable bites are rolled like a Havana cigar, then quick-fried in hot oil. Serve them on a platter lined with shredded lettuce and studded with chopped tomatoes and thinly sliced radishes, cilantro leaves, black olives, pine nuts, sour cream, guacamole, and salsa.

serves 6
45 minutes

1	medium onion, finely chopped
1	small jalapeño pepper, seeded and chopped
1	tablespoon canola oil
2	(4 ounce) boneless, skinless chicken breasts
1	tablespoon water
3	ripe avocados, peeled and thinly sliced
2	cloves garlic
	Juice of 1 lime
	Salt to taste
	Pepper to taste
24	corn tortillas
	Canola (or other vegetable) oil for frying
	Salsa for dipping (see page 14)

1. Preheat a small skillet, then sauté onion in 1 tablespoon hot oil with jalapeño pepper and chicken breast until onion is clear and chicken is cooked, about 5 minutes. Add a tablespoon of water, cover, and simmer 5 minutes.

2. Sprinkle avocado slices with lime juice then strew garlic over all. Cover and set aside.

3. Warm the oven. Preheat a large skillet with about ¾-inch canola or vegetable oil until it's almost smoking. In the meantime, soften tortillas by placing the entire package in the microwave at 100 percent power for 20 seconds. Then assemble the flautas by placing a tablespoon of cooked chicken and onion mixture and an equal amount of guacamole in a line down the middle of each tortilla. Roll like a cigar, then place in hot oil, flap side down, and fry, turning once, until golden, no more than 2 minutes. Cook no more than 3 at a time. Drain on paper towels and hold in the warm oven.

4. Serve hot with salsa for dipping.

Per Serving: 576 calories; 26 g. protein; 34 g. carbohydrate; 43 g. fat; 200 mg. sodium; 76 mg. cholesterol.

Chicken Potato Empanadas

Empanadas are Latin America's hotdog, sold from baskets lined with glistening white cloths at the train station, at soccer games, on street corners. Using a food processor makes this task less labor intensive. Machine chop the vegetables and chicken, mash the potatoes, and make the pastry. To save even more time, start with prepared pie crusts. Serve piping hot with a side of fresh salsa.

8 6-inch pies
45 minutes

Filling

4	chicken thighs *or* 1 7-ounce can cooked chicken
2	medium potatoes, peeled
½	teaspoon salt
1	teaspoon red pepper flakes
3	tablespoons vegetable oil
1	large yellow onion, finely chopped
½	medium green bell pepper, finely chopped
½	medium red bell pepper, finely chopped
1	jalapeño pepper, finely chopped
½	teaspoon ground cumin
½	teaspoon cayenne pepper
1	cup corn, fresh or frozen
8	ounces soft cream cheese
1	cup grated Monterey Jack *or* Mexican white cheese

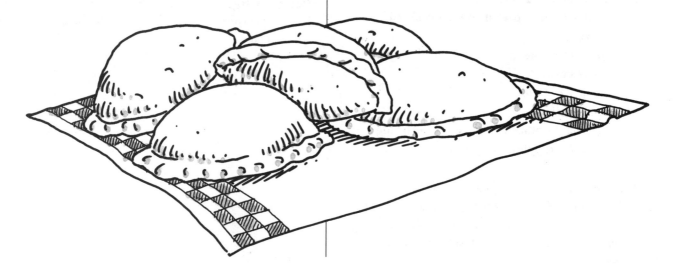

Salt to taste
Freshly ground black pepper to taste

Pastry

1   **cup warm water**
1   **teaspoon white vinegar**
1   **teaspoon salt**
3½ **cups unbleached white flour**
3   **tablespoons vegetable oil**
     Vegetable oil for frying

1. To make filling, combine chicken thighs and potatoes in a medium saucepan with salt and red pepper flakes. Cover with water and boil until chicken and potato are cooked tender, about 20 minutes. Turn off the heat and set aside.

2. While the chicken and potatoes are cooking, heat oil in a 10-inch skillet over medium-high heat. Sauté onions and peppers with cumin and cayenne until vegetables are limp and beginning to brown, about 10 minutes. Add corn and continue cooking for 5 minutes. Remove from heat and stir in cheeses.

3. Lift cooked chicken from cooking water, skin, and debone. Place chicken meat in the food processor fitted with the metal blade. Finely chop the meat, then add it to the cooked vegetables. Place the cooked potatoes in the food processor and puree, then combine with vegetables and meat. Add just enough of the chicken cooking water to make a thick paste. Season to taste with salt and freshly ground black pepper.

4. To make pastry, combine all ingredients in a clean food processor fitted with the metal blade, then process to make a ball that rides the blade around and cleans the sides of the bowl, about 20 seconds.

5. Divide the dough into 8 equal pieces and roll each one out on a lightly floured surface into a 6-inch circle. Place ½ cup of filling on each circle, leaving a ½-inch border. Wet the border to help seal the dough, fold over to form semicircles, and crimp the edges with the tines of a fork.

6. In about an inch of oil heated to 360°F, fry both sides of the pastry until golden, then drain on paper towels.

7. Serve with fresh salsa (see page 14).

Per Serving: 512 calories; 180 g. protein; 115 g. carbohydrate; 38 g. fat; 396 mg. sodium; 66 mg. cholesterol.

Buffalo Chicken Wings

These wings were made popular in the East by college students, who can eat them by the dozen alongside pizza! Good grief. Serve with the traditional accompaniments of celery sticks and blue cheese dressing.

serves 4
30 minutes

1½	**pounds chicken wings, each wing cut into three pieces**
1	**egg, well beaten**
	Canola (or other vegetable) oil for deep frying
1	**3-ounce bottle Louisiana Hot Sauce**
¼	**pound butter or margarine, melted**
	Blue cheese salad dressing
	Celery sticks

1. Coat chicken pieces in beaten egg and set aside.

2. Preheat oil in 10-inch skillet to 360°F.

3. Fry wings in hot oil just until golden, about 5 minutes, then drain on paper towels.

4. Meanwhile, combine hot sauce with butter and dip the chicken wings into it.

5. Serve chicken wings with blue cheese dressing and celery sticks. Dip both chicken and celery in the dressing.

Per Serving: 750 calories; 18 g. protein; 9 g. carbohydrate; 111 g. fat; 1291 mg. sodium; 315 mg. cholesterol.

Sautéed Oysters and Chicken Livers

Serve on a buffet table from a chafing dish. Provide plenty of toothpicks to spear this with and plenty of napkins to dab at the delicious sauce.

makes 40 bites
15 minutes

1	pint fresh oysters
1	pound chicken livers
	Flour
	Salt and Pepper to taste
¼	cup butter or margarine
	Juice and zest of half a lemon
1	tablespoon Worcestershire sauce
¼	cup Madeira

1. Rinse and drain oysters and chicken livers, then dredge in flour. Season to taste with salt and pepper. Heat butter in a large skillet, then sauté until the livers are golden and done and the oysters are bursting and beginning to brown, about 5 minutes.
2. Add lemon juice and zest, Worcestershire sauce, and Madeira and bring to a boil. Once the mixture boils, remove from heat and serve immediately.

Per Serving: 330 calories; 25 g. protein; 15 g. carbohydrate; 17 g. fat; 15 mg. sodium; 301 mg. cholesterol.

Saltimbocca

Saltimbocca means "jumps into the mouth" in Italian. Trust me on this, it's aptly named. Served before dinner on a platter with olives, carrot and celery sticks, Italian peppers, and bread sticks, it's too good an appetizer to waste on company.

serves 2
15 minutes

4	(2 ounce) paper-thin slices cooked chicken breast
4	(2 ounce) paper-thin slices prosciutto or other ham
4	fresh sage leaves
	Freshly ground black pepper
1	tablespoon butter
4	tablespoons Marsala

1. Lay the chicken and ham together, place a sage leaf on top, grate some pepper, roll up, and secure with a toothpick.
2. Heat butter in an 8-inch skillet until it foams. Add meat rolls and brown on all sides, about 5 minutes. Add Marsala, cover, and simmer until wine is absorbed, about 2 minutes. Serve immediately.

Per Serving: 235 calories; 19 g. protein; 11 g. carbohydrate; 13 g. fat; 494 mg. sodium; 80 mg. cholesterol.

Chicken Liver Turnovers

Traditional turnovers are made from handmade short pastry, but you'll save calories and time if you wrap these delicious bites in ready-made won ton skins. The skins can be found in the refrigerated section or produce section of most grocery stores.

60 small turnovers
30 minutes

1	**pound chicken livers**
	Flour
	Salt
	Pepper
¼	**cup butter or margarine**
¼	**cup chopped onion**
	Dash of A-1 sauce
1	**package won ton skins**
1	**tablespoon cornstarch plus water to make a paste**
¼	**cup melted butter or margarine**
	Parmesan cheese
	Paprika

1. Preheat oven to 350°F.
2. Lightly dust chicken livers in flour, salt, and pepper, then sauté over medium-high heat in the butter. When they're about half cooked, add chopped onion, A-1 sauce. Continue cooking until livers are browned and done, about 10 minutes.

3. Remove cooked livers and place in the food processor; pulse to chop finely.
4. To fill the turnovers, make a thin paste from cornstarch and water and wet the edges of each 4-inch-square won ton skin, then place a tablespoon of cooked liver mixture in the middle of each turnover. Fold edges over to form a triangle and press together. Brush with additional melted butter and dust with Parmesan cheese and with a little paprika.
5. Place on lightly greased cookie sheets and bake in the preheated oven until golden brown, about 12 minutes.

Per Serving: 325 calories; 27 g. protein; 35 g. carbohydrate; 21 g. fat; 206 mg. sodium; 232 mg. cholesterol.

Chunky Chicken Sandwich

Here's a sandwich that's terrific in the lunchbox, or as finger sandwiches at high tea. Start with poached chicken breast (see pp 101) or even a can of chicken if you're really pressed for time. Serve with cranberry sauce.

serves 2
10 minutes

2	**(4 ounce) boneless, skinless chicken breasts, poached** *or* **1 cup cooked chicken meat**
4	**slices whole wheat or date-nut bread**
2	**leaves of red tipped lettuce**
2	**tablespoons plain nonfat yogurt**
2	**tablespoons reduced calorie mayonnaise**
1	**stalk celery, finely chopped**
1	**scallion, green and white parts, finely chopped**
3	**tablespoons sweet pickle relish**
2	**tablespoons walnut pieces**
	Salt to taste
	Freshly ground black pepper to taste

1. Cut chicken into small chunks and set aside. Toast bread (optional) and wash and spin dry the lettuce leaves.

2. Combine the remaining ingredients in a bowl then add chicken and season to taste with salt and pepper. Spread chicken mixture onto bread, top with lettuce leaf, and cover with remaining slice of toasted bread.

3. Serve immediately or store in a sealed plastic sandwich bag, refrigerated.

Per Serving: 305 calories; 15 g. protein; 21 g. carbohydrate; 10 g. fat; 586 mg. sodium; 39 mg. cholesterol.

Cranberry Chicken Salad

An American classic, this updated salad can be made anytime since frozen cranberries are available in the supermarket year-round. Use a food processor to chop and puree. Served on a bed of butter lettuce with rich brown bread this makes a fantastic lunch.

serves 6
1 hour

4	**(4 ounce) cooked, boneless, skinless chicken breasts**
1	**stalk celery, finely chopped**
1	**small green apple, cored and chopped**
½	**cup chopped walnuts**
½	**cup reduced-calorie mayonnaise**
8	**ounces plain nonfat yogurt**
½	**teaspoon prepared horseradish**
2	**tablespoons Dijon mustard**
½	**teaspoon whole celery seeds**
1	**cup whole fresh or frozen cranberries**
	A knob of fresh ginger root (about 1 teaspoon)
1	**small orange with peel, seeded and quartered**
	Juice and zest of ½ lemon
1	**teaspoon sugar**

1. Toss cooked chicken, celery, apple, and walnuts together. Set aside.

2. Combine mayonnaise, yogurt, horseradish, mustard, and celery seeds. Set aside.

3. In a food processor fitted with the steel blade coarsely chop the cranberries and ginger, then add the orange. Stir in lemon juice, zest, and sugar until sugar dissolves.

4. Combine cranberry mixture, chicken, and dressing mixture, and toss to mix. Cover and refrigerate at least thirty minutes.

5. Serve on butter lettuce and garnish with additional cranberries and lemon twists.

Per Serving: 301 calories; 17 g. protein; 22 g. carbohydrate; 16 g. fat; 220 mg. sodium; 44 mg. cholesterol.

Tom Parker's Sort-of-Chinese Chicken Salad

Bar none, this is my favorite diet dinner. Strip the chicken skin away if you must, but believe me, the crisp skin of roast chicken is too delicious to sacrifice. Even with skin, this makes a terrific diet lunch. You can begin by roasting a chicken, or buy one already roasted from the deli or grocery store.

serves 4

10 minutes

1	**3 to 4 pound roasted chicken (see page 112)**
1	**head butter or iceberg lettuce**
1	**cup fresh cilantro leaves**
¼	**cup toasted sesame seeds**
1	**tablespoon sesame oil**
	Few drops hot pepper oil
3	**tablespoons rice wine vinegar**
	Salt to taste
	Pepper to taste

1. Bone chicken, discarding bones and any fat. Julienne meat and crisp skin. Cover and keep warm.

2. Break lettuce into bite-sized pieces then place in a large bowl. Add cilantro leaves.

3. Whisk together oils, vinegar, and sesame seeds.

4. Toss hot chicken with chilled greens and dressing, and season to taste with salt and pepper.

5. Mound onto flat dinner plates and serve immediately.

Per Serving: 230 calories; 17 g. protein; 36 g. carbohydrate; 18 g. fat; 105 mg. sodium; 89 mg. cholesterol.

Chicken Stock from Scraps

If you buy a whole chicken, you'll have scraps from which you can make terrific stock to keep on hand in the freezer. Use the chicken back, neck, tail, broken bones, fat, and skin. Not only will you save money by making your own stock, you can also control the salt. Prepared chicken broth has more than 1,000 mg. of sodium. Make it at home and you can leave out the salt entirely, substituting it with a squeeze of lemon juice.

makes 1 quart
30 minutes

1   medium onion, peeled, studded with 4 cloves, and quartered
1   large carrot, broken into pieces
1   stalk celery with leaves, broken into large pieces
1   clove garlic, smashed
2   peppercorns
     Chicken pieces: back, neck, tail, bones, fat, skin
     Quart of cold water
     Salt to taste
     Pepper to taste

1. Simmer ingredients together in a medium stockpot, uncovered, for 1 hour. Taste and adjust seasonings if desired. Squeeze a little lemon juice in if you like. The broth should have some body to it, but doesn't have to taste like finished soup. Think of it as perfumed water.
2. Strain, cool quickly in an ice water bath by placing the bowl in a larger bowl of ice water, then place in pint-sized freezer containers, cover, and freeze. Leave the chicken fat in place because it preserves the broth. Discard fat before use if you wish. Keeps 3 months in the freezer.

Per Serving: 15 calories; 1 g. protein; 1 g. carbohydrate; 1 g. fat; 225 mg. sodium; 1 mg. cholesterol.

• To make chicken noodle or rice soup, simply bring to a boil a pint of homemade chicken broth, chop in celery, onion, and noodles or rice. Cook noodles or rice until done, up to 20 minutes. It's almost a free lunch.
• Want egg drop soup? Whisk in a raw egg just before serving.
• Cook tortellini or ravioli in chicken broth for a quick Italian-style lunch. Dust with Parmesan cheese before serving.
• Make impromptu vegetable soup using bits and pieces of fresh vegetables from your refrigerator. Season to taste with soy sauce. Simmer until the vegetables are soft, about 15 minutes.

Thai Coconut-Chicken Soup

If you can't lay your hands on lemon grass, simply float a whole lemon peel in the soup while it's cooking, then lift it out before serving the soup for that puckery citrus zing.

serves 6
45 minutes

1	pint chicken stock (see page 24)
1	(13 ounce) can coconut milk
1	pint water
	Knob of fresh ginger about as big as your thumb
4	stalks fresh lemon grass, cut into 4-inch lengths *or* lemon peel
12	ounces boneless, skinless chicken thigh meat, cut into ¼-inch-wide strips
4	scallions, green and white parts, cut into 1-inch pieces
1	cup fresh mushrooms, cut into bite-sized pieces
2	tablespoons fresh cilantro
¼	teaspoon crushed red pepper flakes

1. Combine the chicken broth, coconut milk, water, ginger root, and lemon grass or lemon peel in a stockpot. Heat to boiling then reduce heat and simmer for 20 minutes. Remove ginger and lemon grass or lemon peel, and discard.

2. Add chicken, scallions, and mushrooms. Simmer 10 minutes, or until chicken pieces are cooked through. Stir in cilantro and red pepper flakes. Serve hot.

Per Serving: 213 calories; 16 g. protein; 6 g. carbohydrate; 15 g. fat; 466 mg. sodium; 33 mg. cholesterol.

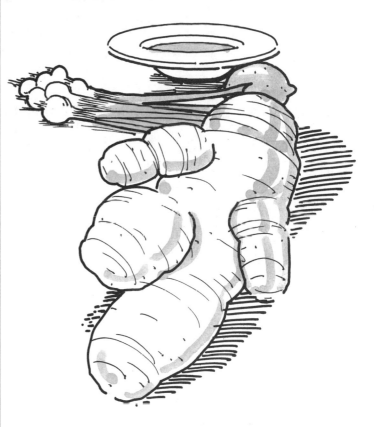

Chapter 2

STIR-FRIED AND SAUTEED
IN A FLASH

Cocky Leeky Chicken with Tomatoes
Sautéed Chicken with Fettucini
Chicken Dijonnaise
Chicken Breast in Mustard-Pistachio Sauce
Chicken Marsala
Chicken Natural
Sautéed Chicken Livers with Chorizo and
Spaghetti
Winter Citrus and Chicken Sauté
Stir-Fried Chicken on Bitter Greens
Garlic Lime Chicken
Lemon Chicken Sauté
Kung Páo Chicken
Chicken San Antone
Ann Greenleaf's Chicken with
Thompson's Grapes
Shredded Chicken, Carrots, and
Green Pepper
Oregon's Own Blueberry Chicken Sauté

HOW TO SAUTE CHICKEN

- Choose a skillet with sloping sides that's large enough that the meat won't be crowded.
- Pound chicken between pieces of waxed paper to a uniform ½-inch thickness.
- Preheat the skillet and oil over medium-high heat before adding the chicken.
- Just before placing the chicken in the skillet, dredge it in seasoned flour and knock off any excess.
- Cook the chicken pieces quickly, about 1 minute per side, turning once or twice. The outside will be sealed by contact with the hot skillet, so the chicken can remain tender with a thin, crisp coating.
- To make a quick sauce after you've removed the chicken from the skillet, swirl a little wine or broth in the pan, scrape up browned bits and stir and reduce the brown, aromatic sauce. Finish with a swirl of butter and cream, or additional chicken broth. Season to taste with salt and pepper.
- Serve sautéed chicken soon after cooking so that the crisp outside and tender inside will remain distinct.

HOW TO STIR-FRY CHICKEN

Stir frying quickly produces a crunchy, crisp-cooked dinner. Success depends upon the technique. Keep the heat high, the batches small, then combine them all just before serving.

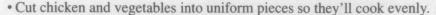

• Cut chicken and vegetables into uniform pieces so they'll cook evenly.

• Prepare all seasonings before you heat the wok or skillet.

• Assemble everything around the wok: chicken, vegetables, sauces, and oils. Once you heat the wok, the cooking goes too fast to hunt for the next item.

• Place a clean, dry wok or large sloping side skillet over high heat. When the wok is hot, add oil (about 2 tablespoons per pound of vegetables and chicken). Heat oil until it ripples when you tilt the wok.

• Add garlic, peppers, or ginger to the wok first to perfume the oil. Toss until light brown, about 30 seconds, then add meat, no more than a half pound at a time. Toss and cook until meat is opaque and beginning to brown, no more than 2 minutes. Remove cooked chicken to a bowl and continue with the next batch of meat or vegetables until you've browned everything, adding a tablespoon of oil from time to time as needed.

• Once vegetables are browned, combine them in the wok, add a table-spoon or so of water, cover, and steam until tender, usually no more than 1 min-ute or so.

• Return cooked meats to the vege-tables in the wok. Add cooking sauce, stir, and cook until the liquid boils and thickens. Scoop the stir-fried food from the wok immediately to a serving bowl.

Cocky Leeky Chicken with Tomatoes

A gratin of potatoes, a tossed green salad, and a loaf of crusty French bread are all you need to make a quick, delightful sauté dinner.

serves 4
30 minutes

4	**(4 ounce) boneless, skinless chicken breasts**
3	**slices thick peppered bacon**
2	**tablespoons butter**
2	**medium leeks, cut in half lengthwise then sliced using 2 inches of green plus the bulb**
½	**cup half and half**
1	**tablespoon chopped fresh tarragon leaves *or* 1 teaspoon dried**
½	**teaspoon red pepper flakes**
6	**Roma *or* 3 medium tomatoes, chopped**
	Salt to taste
	Freshly ground black pepper to taste

1. Flatten chicken breasts between sheets of waxed paper to ½ inch thickness. Set aside.

2. In a 10-inch skillet, cook bacon until crisp, then drain on paper towel. Cook chicken breasts in the bacon fat over medium-high heat until golden brown and fork tender, about 10 minutes. Remove chicken from skillet and reserve.

3. Add butter to skillet, heat, then cook sliced leeks until crisp-tender, about 10 minutes. Stir in half and half, tarragon, and hot pepper flakes. Boil until slightly thickened. Crumble bacon and stir into the sauce. Add tomatoes and chicken. Heat a couple of minutes, until chicken is thoroughly cooked and opaque, then season to taste with salt and pepper.

Per Serving: 465 calories; 44 g. protein; 11 g. carbohydrate; 26 g. fat; 300 mg. sodium; 135 mg. cholesterol.

Sautéed Chicken with Fettucini

We can't decide whether we like this dish best for company or for those private dinners when you can really savor every bite.

serves 4
45 minutes

12	ounces fettucini
3	tablespoons butter
4	(4 ounce) boneless, skinless chicken breasts
2	tablespoons unbleached white flour
3	shallots, minced
⅓	cup parsley, cut fine with scissors
4	cloves garlic, minced
1	teaspoon fresh oregano, minced, *or* ½ teaspoon dried
1	cup brown mushrooms, finely sliced
⅓	cup white wine
½	cup chicken stock (see page 24)
1	medium tomato, finely chopped
3	tablespoons (1 ounce total) feta cheese, crumbled
4	scallions, green and white parts, finely sliced
	Salt to taste
	Freshly ground black pepper to taste

1. Cook fettucini in boiling water to cover until al dente (literally, "to the bite"), about 6 minutes for dried, 1 minute for fresh. Drain in a colander, refresh under cold water, and set aside.

2. While fettucini cooks, heat butter in a 10-inch skillet over medium-high heat. Lightly dredge chicken breasts in flour then brown on both sides. As the meat is cooking toss in shallots, then parsley, garlic, oregano, and mushrooms. Stir in wine, then cover a moment to cook the mushrooms.

3. Remove lid and add chicken stock and chopped tomatoes. Raise heat and stir to reduce sauce by half. Once sauce is reduced, stir in feta cheese and shake pan to melt the cheese into the sauce. Add scallions and cook two or three minutes to soften.

4. Equally distribute cooked fettucini on 4 warmed dinner plates and top with chicken and sauce. Garnish with additional parsley and brown mushrooms.

Per Serving: 447 calories; 34 g. protein; 33 g. carbohydrate; 14 g. fat; 217 mg. sodium; 97 mg. cholesterol.

Chicken Dijonnaise

Nothing more than a toasted baguette is needed to complement this rich, creamy chicken dish. Add a simple composed salad of orange and red onion drizzled with red wine vinaigrette then sprinkled with fresh herbs, and a glass of wine, and you're set.

serves 4

30 minutes

3	tablespoons butter
2	tablespoons unbleached white flour
4	(4 ounce) boneless, skinless chicken breasts
1	medium yellow onion, thinly sliced
1	cup sliced mushrooms
4	cloves garlic, minced
4	artichoke hearts (8 ounces total), canned or frozen
1	cup white wine
2	tablespoons Dijon mustard
½	cup heavy cream
¼	cup finely minced fresh parsley

1. Heat butter in a 10-inch skillet over medium-high heat.

2. Dredge chicken breasts in flour then lightly brown in butter.

3. When you've turned the chicken over, add onion slices, mushrooms, garlic, and artichoke hearts. Sauté, stirring gently, until vegetables become limp and are beginning to brown, about 10 minutes.

4. Combine wine and mustard and add to skillet. Raise heat and boil to reduce by half. Add cream, cook, and stir 3 to 4 more minutes until it becomes a thick, caramel-colored cream.

5. Place breasts on serving dish, top with sauce, and sprinkle with chopped parsley.

Per Serving: 460 calories; 55 g. protein; 42 g. carbohydrate; 26 g. fat; 302 mg. sodium; 142 mg. cholesterol.

Chicken Breast in Mustard-Pistachio Sauce

Quick and easy, this punched-up sauté delivers a lot of taste.

serves 2
20 minutes

2	**(4 ounce) boneless, skinless chicken breasts**
4	**tablespoons unsalted butter or margarine**
	Salt to taste
	Freshly ground black pepper to taste
¼	**teaspoon water**
⅛	**cup Chardonnay (or other dry white wine)**
½	**cup chicken stock (see page 24)**
1	**teaspoon Dijon mustard**
12	**basil leaves *or* 1 teaspoon dried**
½	**cup shelled pistachio nuts**

1. Between sheets of waxed paper, flatten chicken breasts to ½ inch thickness.

2. In an 8-inch skillet over medium heat, heat 2 tablespoons butter until foamy and beginning to brown. Salt and pepper the chicken pieces then place in the skillet. Brown on both sides, then turn the heat down, cover, and steam until done, about 2 minutes per side, adding a quarter teaspoon of water to the skillet after a minute or so. Once chicken is opaque and fork tender, about 10 minutes, remove from the skillet and place on a clean cutting board.

3. Raise heat to high, and add wine and chicken stock. Reduce by half, scraping up bits from the skillet. Season with mustard, 6 basil leaves, and salt and pepper. Whisk in remaining 2 tablespoons butter and half the pistachios, and remove from the heat.

4. Slice chicken breast into thin pieces, make a pool of sauce on each dinner plate and fan the sliced chicken breast on top, garnishing with remaining fresh basil leaves and pistachio nuts.

Per Serving: 307 calories; 31 g. protein; 12 g. carbohydrate; 15 g. fat; 302 mg. sodium; 73 mg. cholesterol.

Chicken Marsala

Marsala, an Italian sweet dessert wine from the town of the same name in Sicily, is a marvelous cooking wine. Unlike sherry, which adds a strong, distinctive flavor to any dish you pour it into, Marsala is more subtle and seems to intensify flavors that were already there. The addition of Marsala can raise quite ordinary sautéed concoctions to new heights.

serves 2
20 minutes

2	**(4 ounce) boneless, skinless chicken breasts**
	Juice and zest from half a lemon
	Flour
	Salt
	Pepper
1	**tablespoon olive oil**
1	**tablespoon butter**
½	**cup fresh mushrooms, sliced**
3	**scallions, green and white parts, finely chopped**
½	**cup Marsala**
2	**teaspoons chopped fresh parsley**

1. Between sheets of waxed paper, flatten chicken breasts into ½-inch-thick fillets. Squeeze lemon juice onto meat. Reserve lemon zest. Lightly dust the fillets with flour, salt, and pepper. Set aside.

2. Heat oil and butter in an 8-inch skillet until butter just begins to turn golden. Quickly sauté the chicken on both sides until golden and done through, about 5 minutes. Remove chicken to a plate and reserve in a warm oven.

3. Add mushrooms and scallions to the skillet and cook, stirring constantly, until browned, about 4 to 5 minutes. Add Marsala and reduce to a thick syrup. Taste and adjust seasonings.

4. Serve by placing a browned chicken fillet on a warm dinner plate, then top with sauce and chopped parsley.

Per Serving: 325 calories; 25 g. protein; 37 g. carbohydrate; 13 g. fat; 66 mg. sodium; 86 mg. cholesterol.

Incorporate this Italian cooking technique into your everyday cooking strategy: Sauté meat, chicken, or vegetables in a little butter mixed with olive oil. Pour in a tablespoon of Marsala and cook until the liquid has been absorbed. Add a modest amount of chicken stock and finish cooking.

Chicken Natural

Sauté this chicken in anything less than butter and you'll compromise the flavor. Once in a while, there's just nothing like the taste of pure butter.

serves 4
45 minutes

1	3 to 4 pound frying chicken, cut into serving pieces
4	tablespoons butter
1	medium onion, thinly sliced
1	green pepper, chopped
2	cloves garlic, pressed
2	medium tomatoes, quartered
	Salt to taste
	Pepper to taste
4	ounces mozzarella cheese, sliced
1	teaspoon capers
	Anchovy fillets
	Parsley, cut fine with scissors

1. In a 10-inch skillet over medium-high heat sauté chicken in butter until golden all over, about 5 minutes. Set aside on a clean plate. Cover.

2. Sauté onion, pepper, and garlic in the skillet just until onion is clear, about 5 minutes. Add tomatoes. Replace chicken atop the vegetables. Season to taste with salt and pepper. Cover skillet tightly, lower heat, and cook until chicken is fork tender, about 20 minutes.

3. Just before serving, lay mozzarella slices on chicken pieces, sprinkle with capers, and layer anchovy fillets on top. Garnish with parsley. Cover and let the cheese melt before serving.

Per Serving: 346 calories; 42 g. protein; 9 g. carbohydrate; 15 g. fat; 291 mg. sodium; 105 mg. cholesterol.

Sautéed Chicken Livers with Chorizo and Spaghetti

Mexican chorizo sausage is available in supermarkets where Mexican foods can be found. You can substitute bulk breakfast sausage. A side dish of roasted red peppers makes a gorgeous plate.

serves 4
1 hour

1	medium yellow onion, finely chopped
1	tablespoon olive oil
¼	pound chorizo sausage, casings removed
1	head garlic, cloves peeled and minced
1	pound chicken livers
	Flour seasoned with salt and pepper
1	teaspoon fresh thyme
½	teaspoon dried sage
½	teaspoon ground allspice
	Juice and zest of 1 lemon
	Salt to taste
	Pepper to taste
12	ounces fresh fettucini
	Lemon slices (garnish)
	Sprigs of fresh herb (garnish)

1. Sauté the onion in oil until translucent. Add sausage and cook until nearly done, about 10 minutes, stirring from time to time. Add minced garlic and cook 2 more minutes. Lift mixture from the skillet and reserve.

2. Dredge chicken livers in flour then sauté them in the pan juices until golden, about 5 minutes. Return the sausage mixture to the pan and toss well with the livers. Add herbs, allspice, and lemon juice and zest.
3. Meanwhile, cook pasta according to package directions. Drain and toss with a dash of olive oil. Arrange pasta into a nest on a serving platter, top with the livers and squeeze, and garnish with slices of lemon and sprigs of fresh herbs.

Per Serving: 415 calories; 27 g. protein; 46 g. carbohydrate; 15 g. fat; 710 mg. sodium; 265 mg. cholesterol.

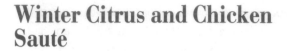

Winter Citrus and Chicken Sauté

Use only the sweetest ruby red grapefruit and good juice oranges for this winter sauté. Served over a bed of mixed brown rice, this makes a colorful, zesty entree.

serves 4
45 minutes

2   juice oranges
2   ruby red grapefruit
4   (4 ounce) boneless, skinless chicken breasts
2   tablespoons unbleached white flour
     Salt to taste

Cayenne to taste
Freshly ground black pepper to taste
1   tablespoon olive oil
1   leek, trimmed to include 1 inch of green, then quartered and thoroughly washed to remove sand
¼   cup dry vermouth *or* other dry white wine
2   tablespoons orange marmalade
2   tablespoons minced chives
     Orange zest (garnish)

1. Using a sharp knife, remove skin and pith from oranges and grapefruit. Cut strips of zest from one orange and reserve for garnish. Then, holding fruit over a bowl to catch the juice, cut away membrane and seeds, dividing the fruit into segments. Measure juice and add water to make ½ cup. Set citrus segments and juice aside.

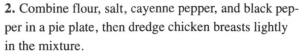

2. Combine flour, salt, cayenne pepper, and black pepper in a pie plate, then dredge chicken breasts lightly in the mixture.

3. Heat a 10-inch skillet over medium-high heat, then add oil. Sauté chicken breasts, 3 to 4 minutes per side, or until cooked golden on the outside and opaque white throughout. Set chicken breasts onto a warm plate and reserve.

4. Cut leeks into 2-inch-long pieces, then cook them in the same skillet, adding a teaspoon more oil if the skillet is dry, stirring until soft and beginning to brown on the edges, 3 to 5 minutes. Add reserved fruit juices and vermouth and raise to a boil. Boil until the liquid is reduced by half.

5. Lower the heat and stir in marmalade. Add the fruit and chicken, stir to coat, then sprinkle with chives. Taste and adjust seasonings if necessary. Heat chicken and fruit.

6. To serve, pool the citrus sauce on a dinner plate. Place hot sautéed chicken and fruit on top of sauce and garnish with reserved orange zest.

Per Serving: 314 calories; 35 g. protein; 26 g. carbohydrate; 9 g. fat; 81 mg. sodium; 73 mg. cholesterol.

Stir-Fried Chicken on Bitter Greens

Serve this Thai-style stir fry alongside seasonal sweet fresh fruit.

serves 4
30 minutes

4   cups bitter salad greens: any mixture of watercress, arugula, Belgian endive, bok choy, spinach, rinsed and spun dry
1   tablespoon rice vinegar

Sauce

2   cloves garlic, pressed
½   teaspoon sugar
3   tablespoons dry sherry
3   tablespoons Thai fish sauce (available in Asian markets or gourmet food stores)
½   teaspoon grated fresh ginger
4   (4 ounce) boneless, skinless chicken breasts
2   tablespoons peanut (or other bland) cooking oil
1   medium onion, peeled, quartered, and divided into single layers

1. Compose the greens onto four dinner plates, drizzle with rice vinegar, and set aside.
2. Combine sauce ingredients, except for oil and onion, in a small bowl and set aside.

3. Flatten chicken breasts between sheets of waxed paper to ¼ inch thick. Remove paper and cut the meat across the grain into 1-inch-wide strips.

4. Place the wok over high heat. When it's hot, add 1 tablespoon oil and the onion. Stir fry until onion edges begin to brown. Scoop the onion into a bowl and reserve.

5. Add remaining tablespoon oil to the wok, then the chicken. Stir fry until the chicken begins to brown on the edges and is thoroughly opaque and done through, about 2 minutes. Scoop the chicken into the bowl with the onion.

6. Remove the wok from the heat, add sauce, then stir to free browned bits. Place the wok over high heat, add chicken and onions, and stir until the sauce boils nearly dry.

7. Spoon the chicken and onion mixture on top of the arranged greens. Garnish with fresh seasonal fruit and serve immediately.

Per Serving: 225 calories; 28 g. protein; 5 g. carbohydrate; 8.5 g. fat; 575 mg. sodium; 73 mg. cholesterol.

For an interesting variation, wilt the greens in the oiled hot wok for just a minute or two, toss with rice vinegar, then divide among the dinner plates.

Garlic Lime Chicken

This preparation is equally good sautéed or grilled. Quick-marinate the meat in the refrigerator a half hour, then depending on the weather, cook it indoors or out.

serves 4
1 hour

4	**(4 ounce) boneless, skinless chicken breasts**
½	**cup low-sodium soy sauce**
	Juice and zest of a lime
1	**tablespoon Worcestershire sauce**
2	**cloves garlic, minced**
½	**teaspoon dry mustard**
½	**teaspoon freshly ground black pepper**
	Zest of one lime (garnish)

1. Flatten chicken breasts between sheets of waxed paper to ½ inch thickness.
2. Combine soy sauce, lime juice and zest, Worcestershire sauce, garlic, and mustard in a glass dish. Add chicken, turn it, cover, and refrigerate for 30 minutes.
3. Remove chicken from the marinade and pepper it. Discard the marinade. Add just enough oil to a skillet to cover the bottom, then heat over medium-high heat.
4. Cook chicken until golden on both sides and opaque and done, about 10 minutes.

5. Serve hot or at room temperature. Garnish with additional lime zest if you wish.

Per Serving: 130 calories; 25 g. protein; 1 g. carbohydrate; 2 g. fat; 489 mg. sodium; 73 mg. cholesterol.

Lemon Chicken Sauté

The flavor of chicken combined with lemon makes a quick, satisfying sauté you can have on the table in no time.

serves 4
15 minutes

4	**(4 ounce) boneless, skinless chicken breasts**
	Paprika
	Dash of olive oil or vegetable cooking spray
1	**tablespoon olive oil**
1	**teaspoon butter**
2	**cups (½ pound) fresh mushrooms, finely chopped**
1½	**teaspoons fresh minced tarragon *or* ¾ teaspoon dried**
2	**tablespoons minced fresh parsley**
	Juice and zest of ½ lemon

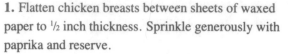

1. Flatten chicken breasts between sheets of waxed paper to ½ inch thickness. Sprinkle generously with paprika and reserve.

2. Heat a 10-inch skillet over medium-high heat then add just enough oil or cooking spray to cover the bottom. Sauté breasts until golden on both sides, about 5 minutes. Remove to a warmed plate.

3. Combine oil and butter in the skillet. Add mushrooms, herbs, and lemon juice and zest. Cover and cook over medium heat until the mushrooms are reduced and beginning to brown. Place the breasts back in the skillet and cook until done, about 10 minutes.

4. To serve, arrange on dinner plates and garnish with additional twists of lemon peel.

Per Serving: 305 calories; 27 g. protein; 2 g. carbohydrate; 9 g. fat; 64 mg. sodium; 73 mg. cholesterol.

Kung Paó Chicken

One of the best-loved Szechuan dishes on America's West Coast, it's a meal in itself when paired with fluffy white rice. If you don't have a wok, use your biggest skillet.

serves 4
30 minutes

4	(4 ounce) boneless, skinless chicken breasts
2	tablespoons soy sauce
3	tablespoons cornstarch
1	green bell pepper, julienned
2	stalks celery, chopped on the diagonal
2	scallions, green and white parts, chopped
1	tablespoon peanut (or vegetable) oil
8	medium dried red peppers
½	cup roasted peanuts

Seasoning Sauce

4	tablespoons soy sauce
2	tablespoons dry sherry
2	tablespoons rice wine vinegar
2	tablespoons sugar
2	teaspoons sesame oil

1. Cut chicken into bite-sized pieces and place in a glass bowl.

2. Mix soy sauce and cornstarch into a smooth paste and combine with the chicken. Stir to coat all pieces, cover, and set aside 10 minutes.

3. After cutting the vegetables, make the seasoning sauce. Combine all ingredients in a small bowl and set aside.

4. Preheat the wok over high heat until a drop of water flicked onto it leaps off.

5. Heat oil in the hot wok, then fry red peppers until blackened, about 1 minute. Add chicken pieces and stir fry just until chicken begins to brown, about 2 minutes. Add green pepper and celery and stir fry until crunchy—no more than 2 minutes.

6. Add seasoning sauce and stir until thickened and hot—just a minute or so. Remove from the heat and stir in peanuts and scallions. Mix together and serve, either with rice or noodles.

Per Serving: 296 calories; 31 g. protein; 9 g. carbohydrate; 12 g. fat; 1163 mg. sodium; 73 mg. cholesterol.

Chicken San Antone

Here's a one-dish diet dinner that does everything: pleases the eye, satisfies the appetite, and is on the table in 30 minutes.

serves 2
30 minutes

1	tablespoon olive oil
2	(4 ounce) boneless, skinless chicken breasts
	Salt
	Pepper
1	medium onion
1	fresh jalapeño pepper, seeded
6	cloves garlic
1	stalk celery
1	cup cherry tomatoes
1	ear of corn, cut from cob (about 1 cup of kernels)
	Juice and zest from ½ lime
1	tablespoon chili powder
1	small head romaine lettuce
	Black olives (garnish)

1. Heat a 10-inch skillet over medium-high heat, then add oil. Season chicken breasts with salt and pepper, then sauté until golden brown on both sides, about 10 minutes.

2. Meanwhile, finely chop the onion, jalapeño pepper, garlic, and celery. Set aside. In a food processor fitted with the steel blade, puree the tomatoes, then stir in the corn kernels, lime juice, and chili powder and set aside.

3. Once chicken is cooked, lift it from the skillet and set aside on a clean dish. Add the onion-garlic mixture to the skillet and saute until onion is translucent, about 5 minutes. Pour in tomato and corn mixture, place chicken on top, cover, and cook for about 10 minutes. Season to taste with salt and pepper.

4. Divide lettuce evenly between two dinner plates. Scoop vegetable and chicken mixture on top of each one, garnish with a black olive, and serve.

Per Serving: 286 calories; 32 g. protein; 31 g. carbohydrate; 10 g. fat; 526 mg. sodium; 73 mg. cholesterol.

Ann Greenleaf's Chicken with Thompson's Grapes

Ann's been serving this festive dish from a black skillet to friends for twenty years. It looks good, tastes good, and is so easy to make that you can spend most of your time before dinner visiting with your guests while it cooks. Ann says she's tried this with fresh grapes but they're too watery and don't taste any better, and flame grapes turn a ghastly color. So, my friend Ann says, stick to canned Thompson's seedless grapes for best results.

serves 4
45 minutes

4   (4 ounce) boneless, skinless chicken breasts
2   tablespoons white, unbleached flour
    Nutmeg to taste
    Salt to taste
    Pepper to taste
2   tablespoons water
2   tablespoons olive oil
2   tablespoons apricot preserves
1   (20 ounce) can Thompson's seedless grapes
    Chinese hot mustard

1. Cut chicken breasts into finger-wide strips, then dredge in flour, nutmeg, salt, and pepper.

2. Heat oil in a cast-iron black skillet over medium heat, then brown chicken pieces on all sides. Cover, lower the heat, add 2 tablespoons of water, and cook until done, about 10 minutes, checking to make sure it's not sticking. Add water or juice from the grapes as needed.

3. Lift chicken from the skillet and put on a clean plate. Scrape up browned bits from the skillet and combine with apricot preserves. Stir and add ¼ cup water or juice from the grapes to make a glaze. Return chicken to the skillet and stir to coat.

4. Drain grapes and add to the skillet. Heat through. Serve the chicken from the skillet with brown rice and Chinese hot mustard.

Per Serving: 310 calories; 35 g. protein; 24 g. carbohydrate; 8 g. fat; 120 mg. sodium; 73 mg. cholesterol.

Shredded Chicken, Carrots, and Green Pepper

Bright colors, crunchy vegetables, and quickly stir-fried chicken make this an easy dish to make for dinner. Serve with fluffy white rice.

serves 4
30 minutes

4	**(4 ounce) boneless, skinless chicken breasts**
4	**teaspoons cornstarch**
2	**teaspoons soy sauce**
2	**tablespoons dry sherry**
1	**large egg white, beaten until foamy**
1	**tablespoon peanut (or vegetable) oil**
1	**carrot, scraped clean, then shredded**
1	**green pepper, seeded and cut into strips**
1	**teaspoon fresh ginger, shredded**
1	**scallion, white and green parts, cut into ½-inch pieces**
1	**teaspoon sugar**
2	**tablespoons cold water**

1. Use a fillet knife to slice chicken breast horizontally into paper-thin slices. Stack the slices and cut into ⅛-inch-wide strips. Place the chicken in a bowl.

2. Combine 2 teaspoons cornstarch and 2 teaspoons soy sauce with the sherry and egg white. Pour over the chicken and rub into all strips. Cover and refrigerate for about 30 minutes.

3. Heat 1 teaspoon oil in a wok and add the carrots for 1 minute. Add green pepper and continue to stir fry another minute. Remove carrots and peppers.

4. Heat remaining 2 teaspoons of oil and stir fry ginger and scallion for 30 seconds. Using a slotted spoon, lift chicken shreds from marinade and add to the wok, stir frying until chicken turns white and opaque and begins to brown on the edges, about 2 minutes. Add reserved vegetables, sugar, and remaining soy sauce. Cook until heated through.

5. Meanwhile, combine remaining cornstarch with cold water. Stir into wok and cook until clear. Serve.

Per Serving: 275 calories; 72 g. protein; 26 g. carbohydrate; 5 g. fat; 56 mg. sodium; 85 mg. cholesterol.

Oregon's Own Blueberry Chicken Sauté

Marsha Johnson makes the sauce for this sauté using her own handmade vinegar for the reduction. For the most luxurious presentation, pool this purple-blue sauce on a white serving platter and top with the chicken breasts.

serves 4
30 minutes

4	(4 ounce) boneless, skinless chicken breasts
2	tablespoons unsalted butter
¼	cup finely minced shallots
4	tablespoons blueberry vinegar (preferably "Oregon's Own")
¼	cup chicken stock (see page 24)
¼	cup whipping cream

1	tablespoon finely minced tomato
½	cup fresh blueberries (garnish)

1. In a 10-inch skillet, sauté breasts in butter over medium-high heat, turning frequently, until golden brown on all sides and opaque, about 10 minutes.
2. Remove breasts to a warmed platter and reserve. Add shallots to the skillet and sauté 2 minutes, then raise the heat and add vinegar. Boil and reduce to 1 tablespoon. Add stock, whipping cream, and tomato. Cook and stir a moment. Season to taste with salt and pepper.
3. To serve, pool sauce on the platter, then top with cooked chicken breast and reserved blueberries. Serve immediately.

Per Serving: 408 calories; 54 g. protein; 8 g. carbohydrate; 17 g. fat; 395 mg. sodium; 154 mg. cholesterol.

Chapter 3

QUICK-GRILLED AND MICROWAVED CHICKEN

Quick Chicken Piquant
Lemon Micro-Barbecued Chicken
Chicken Micro-Poached in Orange Juice
Charcoal-Grilled Sesame-Soy
Chicken Wings
Chicken Stroganoff
Grilled Chicken Breast with Green Sauce
Korean-Style Barbecue
Grilled Chili Chicken with Couscous
Wally Dysert's Worcestershire
Grilled Chicken
Diana's Grilled Blackberry Chicken
Pollo El Paso

INCREASING THE SAFETY OF
BARBECUED CHICKEN

It's not enough that we have to worry about how to feed the family without breaking the bank, but now we have to look at every food item as if it were a deadly poison.

Take barbecued chicken. Long considered a good, cheap meal for a crowd, this all-American favorite has come in for some heavy criticism lately. Salmonella and campylobacter outbreaks perfectly parallel the beginning of the outdoor cooking season, and mishandled, undercooked chicken takes the blame. If bacteria from raw birds gets transferred to cutting boards, knives, bowls, and marinades, you're likely to get sick.

Remember that you've got to wash your hands, cutting boards, and knives with hot soapy water, and discard the marinade once you start barbecuing the bird. Baste with fresh sauce, and cook that bird until it's done. How can you tell? Cut into a piece. The flesh should be opaque white, never pinkish. Juices should run clear, never pinkish. Bones won't look red in thoroughly cooked chicken. If you press your finger into the flesh it will feel "seized," as the French say, like a tensed muscle, not mushy and flaccid.

Did I mention cancer? We've all heard that carcinogens float up from the smoke into barbecued foods and can settle in our bodies. What actually happens is that cooking meat, chicken, or fish at high temperatures—barbecue, frying, or broiling—produces heterocyclic aromatic amines, which cause cancer in laboratory animals. Meats cooked at lower temperatures—microwaved, stewed, poached, or boiled—produce virtually none of these chemicals. What can you do?

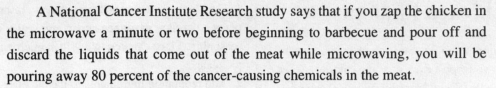

A National Cancer Institute Research study says that if you zap the chicken in the microwave a minute or two before beginning to barbecue and pour off and discard the liquids that come out of the meat while microwaving, you will be pouring away 80 percent of the cancer-causing chemicals in the meat.

One last thing. Enjoy your summer barbecue. Don't look at everything on your plate as if it were poison. If you cooked it yourself and used common sense plus a shot of scientific data, you will have a perfectly nutritious, delicious dinner.

Quick Chicken Piquant

A diet dinner in no time, this chicken packs such a flavor punch you won't even miss the calories. Serve on a bed of noodles if you like (this adds 100 calories per serving).

serves 2
20 minutes

2	**(4 ounce) boneless, skinless chicken breasts**
	Salt to taste
	Pepper to taste
	Paprika to taste
	Cayenne pepper to taste
	Italian dried herbs to taste
1½	**cups chopped brown mushrooms**
2	**cups total chopped red and green bell peppers**
½	**cup chopped parsley**
1	**cup minced fresh tomato**
12	**whole black seedless olives**
12	**fresh basil leaves *or* 1 teaspoon dried**

1. Cut chicken into strips then season to taste with salt, pepper, paprika, cayenne pepper, and Italian dried herb seasoning. Place chicken in a 9-inch microwaveable pie plate.

2. Add remaining ingredients to the pie plate, cover tightly with microwave plastic wrap, taking care that the plastic doesn't touch the meat, and place it in the microwave.

3. Microwave at 100 percent (full) power for 5 minutes then let it stand for five minutes.

4. While the chicken and vegetables are cooking, cook noodles according to package directions (if you wish). Drain the noodles and arrange in the bottom of two soup bowls.

5. Serve chicken and vegetables over the noodles and garnish with fresh basil and a grating of black pepper.

Per Serving: 234 calories; 43 g. protein; 11 g. carbohydrate; 9 g. fat; 202 mg. sodium; 73 mg. cholesterol.

Lemon Micro-Barbecued Chicken

Precooking chicken in the microwave for a minute or two brings about reduction of the potentially carcinogenic chemicals produced by cooking meat at high temperatures.

If you want to feel safe about your barbecue and don't want to worry about heterocyclic aromatic amines, zap chicken in the microwave to start, then discard the liquid that oozes out.

serves 8 people
1 hour plus marinating overnight

2	**(3 to 4 pound) chickens, quartered**
1½	**cups canola oil**
	Juice and zest of 2 lemons
2	**cloves garlic, pressed**
2	**tablespoons fresh onion, minced**
1	**teaspoon fresh thyme, crushed,** *or* ½ **teaspoon dried**
2	**tablespoons fresh parsley, snipped,** *or* **2 teaspoons dried**
2	**tablespoons fresh sweet basil, snipped,** *or* **2 teaspoons dried**
1	**teaspoon salt**
1	**teaspoon paprika**
¼	**teaspoon cayenne**

1. Place quartered chicken in shallow glass baking dish.

2. Whisk together the remaining ingredients. Reserve 1 cup of the marinade in a covered jar in the refrigerator. Pour remaining marinade over the chicken, cover, and refrigerate overnight, turning the chicken occasionally.

3. About an hour before serving time, build a charcoal fire in a covered grill and heat until coals are covered with white ash (or preheat a gas grill 5 minutes).

4. Lift chicken from marinade, and discard this marinade. Place chicken in a microwave dish, cover with plastic wrap, and microwave on 100 percent (full) power for 1 minute. Discard the liquid that secretes from the chicken.

5. Cook chicken on the grill, brushing frequently with the reserved marinade from the jar. Turn the chicken often and cook until the bird is golden brown and cooked through, about 30 minutes. Serve immediately.

Per Serving: 140 calories; 27 g. protein; 0 g. carbohydrate; 3 g. fat; 64 mg. sodium; 73 mg. cholesterol.

Chicken Micro-Poached in Orange Juice

Poach everybody's favorite pieces for this easy supper. Couscous on the side and steamed artichokes make this meal complete.

serves 4
45 minutes

4 to 6	pieces of chicken (your choice)
	Salt to taste
	Freshly ground black pepper to taste
	Red pepper to taste
	White pepper to taste
²/₃	cup fresh orange juice
½	cup dry white wine
1	teaspoon cornstarch
1	carrot, scraped and julienned
1	large onion, peeled and thinly sliced
2	stalks celery, cut on the diagonal into small pieces
1	teaspoon dried Italian herbs
1	orange, peeled and sectioned (garnish)

1. Arrange chicken pieces in a microwave dish with the thicker parts toward the edge. Season to taste with salt and peppers.

2. Combine orange juice and wine with cornstarch and mix. Pour it over the chicken. Arrange carrots, onions, and celery over the chicken and sprinkle with Italian herbs. Cover tightly with microwave plastic wrap, taking care that plastic doesn't touch the meat.

3. Microwave at 100 percent (full) power in the microwave for 15 minutes, turning the dish once, halfway through the cooking. Carefully remove wrap and check to see that chicken pieces are cooked through. Let the chicken stand for 5 minutes before serving.

4. To serve, place a spoonful of couscous or rice on the plate, then spoon chicken and sauce over. Garnish with additional orange slices.

Per Serving: 297 calories; 19 g. protein; 13 g. carbohydrate; 5 g. fat; 66 mg. sodium; 73 mg. cholesterol.

Charcoal-Grilled Sesame-Soy Chicken Wings

If your supermarket carries first joint chicken wings sometimes sold as drumettes, buy those. Otherwise, buy a larger amount of three-part chicken wings and cut off the tip section and toss that into a pot for stock. (See index). If you have a hibachi, this is an ideal recipe to use. For a party, double, triple, or quadruple the recipe, then cover the top of the hibachi with these sherry-soy drenched wings. You'll have instant hot-off-the-grill hors d'oeuvres.

serves 4

30 minutes, plus marinating overnight

2   **pounds chicken wings (baby drumsticks, or drumettes)**
4   **tablespoons soy sauce**
1   **cup dry sherry**
4   **tablespoons sugar**
     Knob of ginger the size of your thumb, grated
2   **teaspoons hot sesame oil**
2   **tablespoons toasted sesame seeds**

1. Arrange chicken wings in a flat glass dish.

2. Combine all ingredients except sesame seeds in a small jar, shake to mix, then pour half over the chicken. Cover and marinate overnight. Keep reserved marinade in the refrigerator.

3. In a hibachi or charcoal grill, build a fire about 45 minutes before serving time. Once coals are glowing, lift wings from the marinade and arrange them close together on the grill. Discard marinade.

4. Baste the chicken pieces with reserved marinade, turning the pieces from time to time until they're cooked through and golden grown. Douse any flame-ups with a spray of plain water.

5. To serve, arrange wings on a platter and sprinkle with toasted sesame seeds.

Per Serving: 285 calories; 13 g. protein; 6 g. carbohydrate; 13 g. fat; 820 mg. sodium; 146 mg. cholesterol.

Marinade Safety Tip: Always discard marinade you have soaked poultry in before you begin cooking. Baste the birds with marinade you've reserved in a jar—or with fresh oil. Remember that harmful bacteria can transfer from raw poultry to the marinade during the soaking time.

Chicken Stroganoff

Serve with our version of stroganoff with steamed broccoli, your family's favorite fruit salad, and some dark bread.

serves 4
45 minutes

4	**(5 ounce) boneless, skinless chicken thighs**
½	**cup water**
1	**medium onion, chopped**
½	**cup mushrooms, chopped**
2	**cloves garlic, pressed**
3	**tablespoons margarine or butter**
2	**tablespoons unbleached flour**
1	**cup milk**
1	**(4 ounce) jar pimientos**
½	**teaspoon chopped fresh thyme leaves *or* a pinch dried**
	Salt to taste
	Pepper to taste
1	**(10 ounce) package fresh spinach *or* egg noodles**
1	**cup sour cream**
	Parsley sprigs (garnish)

1. Place chicken pieces in a microwaveable dish. Add ½ cup water, cover, and microwave at 100 percent (full) power for 15 minutes. Let chicken stand 5 minutes, then cut into bite-sized pieces.

2. While chicken is cooking, sauté onion, mushrooms, and garlic in 2 tablespoons margarine in a 10-inch skillet, about 5 minutes, or until onion is beginning to brown. Sprinkle with flour and stir to coat. Pour in the milk, add pimiento and thyme leaves, then cook and stir until sauce is thick. Season to taste with salt and pepper. Stir in cooked chicken.

3. At the same time, cook noodles according to package directions, until *al dente*. Drain, and toss with margarine.

4. To serve, stir sour cream into sauce, then pour over the noodles. Garnish with fresh parsley sprigs and serve hot.

Per Serving: 465 calories; 23 g. protein; 41 g. carbohydrate; 23 g. fat; 365 mg. sodium; 105 mg. cholesterol.

Grilled Chicken Breast with Green Sauce

Pretty as a picture, fanned slices of golden grilled chicken with a green sauce and roasted red potatoes makes a brightly flavored dinner that feeds the eyes.

serves 2
1 hour

2   **(4 ounce) boneless, skinless chicken breasts**
       Salt to taste
       Freshly ground black pepper to taste

Sauce

1   **cup Italian flat leaf parsley, coarsely chopped**
2   **cloves garlic, minced**
4   **anchovy fillets, minced**
2   **tablespoons sun-dried tomatoes, minced**
1   **tablespoon roasted red pepper, minced**
¾   **cup olive oil**
3   **tablespoons balsamic vinegar**
       Salt to taste
       Pepper to taste

1. Preheat the grill.

2. Season chicken to taste with salt and pepper.

3. Combine sauce ingredients in a jar, cover, and shake. Let sauce stand while you're grilling. This sauce will keep up to a week in the refrigerator.

4. Grill chicken breasts until golden and done, with appropriate cross-hatched grill marks, about 3 minutes per side.

5. To serve, slice each breast into thin pieces. Place a pool of green sauce on each plate then fan the meat out on the plate. Roasted red potatoes and sautéed zucchini shards make ideal accompaniments.

Per Serving: 250 calories; 27 g. protein; 8 g. carbohydrate; 8 g. fat; 64 mg. sodium; 73 mg. cholesterol.

To roast red potatoes, preheat the oven to 400°F. Quarter potatoes then toss with olive oil, salt, pepper, and paprika to taste. Roast, stirring from time to time until potatoes are tender throughout and crisp golden brown on the outside, about 20 minutes.

Korean-Style Barbecue

Precook chicken in the microwave, then grill it over glowing coals and you're guaranteed chicken that's cooked through, fork tender, and mouth-watering with the taste of woodsmoke. Leave the skin and bones on the bird for best results.

Marinate these chicken pieces overnight and the sweet-sour-salty taste will go clear through to the bone. Remember to pour out the marinade before you begin cooking.

serves 6
45 minutes, plus marinating overnight

4   chicken drumstick and thigh sections,
     cut in 2 pieces
1   whole breast, cut in 2 pieces

Marinade

1   cup soy sauce
     Juice and zest of 2 lemons
1/2   cup water
1   cup sugar
1/2   cup sesame oil (available in Asian markets or
     the Oriental section of most grocery stores)
4   cloves garlic, pressed
2   tablespoons grated onion
2   tablespoons grated fresh ginger

1. In a microwaveable dish arrange chicken pieces in a spoke pattern with the thickest pieces on the outside edges. Combine marinade ingredients, reserving half in a covered jar in the refrigerator. Pour remaining marinade over the chicken, cover with plastic wrap, and marinate overnight. Turn the chicken pieces occasionally.

2. About an hour before serving, prepare a charcoal fire for grilling. Just before cooking, drain and discard the marinade from the chicken.

3. Recover the chicken and microwave at 100 percent (full) power for 5 minutes. Drain and discard the juice.

4. Immediately place the chicken on the grill, about 6 inches above the glowing coals. Brush with the reserved marinade, then cook, turning from time to time with tongs, brushing frequently with the marinade, until the chicken is golden brown, fork tender, and the juices run clear when pierced with a fork, about 20 minutes.

Per Serving: 180 calories; 22 g. protein; 5 g. carbohydrate; 8 g. fat; 750 mg. sodium; 65 mg. cholesterol.

Grilled Chili Chicken with Couscous

The thing I love about couscous is that it cooks in less than 5 minutes and makes a comforting bed for many a quick-grilled chicken dish. You can either grill this chicken over charcoal, or, in a pinch, sauté it in a pan. Either way, you get a glorious golden bed of couscous, a delicious breast of chicken, and a dazzling red pepper sauce. Sautéed mushrooms and Italian parsley finish the plate. All you need add to make this menu complete is a loaf of crusty French bread and a tossed green salad.

serves 4
30 minutes

4   **(4 ounce) boneless, skinless chicken breasts**
     Salt to taste
     Cayenne pepper to taste
     Freshly ground black pepper to taste
1   **tablespoon olive oil**

Chili Pepper Sauce

1   **(7 ounce) jar roasted red peppers, drained**
3   **cloves garlic**
¼   **cup onion**
     Juice of half a lemon
1   **teaspoon chili powder**
     Salt to taste
     Pepper to taste

Couscous

1	cup couscous
1½	cups boiling water
1	tablespoon butter
¼	teaspoon salt
2	tablespoons minced chives
2	tablespoons toasted pine nuts

Garnish

2	cups fresh mushrooms
1	tablespoon olive oil
	Italian parsley sprigs

1. About 45 minutes before serving time, build a charcoal fire in a grill or hibachi. Flatten chicken breasts between sheets of wax paper to ½ inch thickness. Season to taste with salt, cayenne, and black pepper. Drizzle the meat with olive oil, cover, and set aside while fire preheats.

2. In a blender or food processor combine roasted red peppers, garlic, onion, lemon juice, and chili powder. Process until smooth, season to taste with salt and pepper, and set aside, covered.

3. Stir couscous into 1½ cups boiling water with butter and salt, cover, and let stand 10 minutes. Fluff with a fork. Stir in chives and pine nuts and set aside.

4. Meanwhile, in a 10-inch skillet, sauté mushrooms in olive oil, just until soft. Set aside.

5. Grill chicken breasts about 3 inches above the glowing coals, just until opaque and grill marks show, no more than 3 to 5 minutes per side. Remove from grill and place on a warm serving plate.

6. To serve, place a scoop of couscous on a dinner plate, top with a grilled chicken breast and a dollop of chili sauce. Finish with sautéed mushrooms on the side and a sprig of parsley on top.

Per Serving: 485 calories; 39 g. protein; 38 g. carbohydrate; 18 g. fat; 83 mg. sodium; 82 mg. cholesterol.

Wally Dysert's Worcestershire Grilled Chicken

Easy and good, this crisp mahogany-flavored grilled chicken can be made with chicken parts or whole, quartered birds. You could—for sheer perfection—rotisserie a whole bird.

serves 4
45 minutes, plus marinating overnight

1	**(3 to 4 pound) chicken, quartered**
	Worcestershire sauce
	Coarsely ground black pepper
	Butter or margarine

1. Place chicken in a shallow glass baking dish. Douse the bird on all sides with Worcestershire sauce. Pepper generously, then cover and refrigerate overnight.

2. About an hour before serving time, build a charcoal fire in a covered grill and heat until coals are covered with white ash (or preheat a gas grill 5 minutes).

3. Melt a little butter and give it a generous shot of fresh Worcestershire.

4. Lift chicken from marinade, and discard any remaining liquid. Cook chicken on the grill, brushing frequently with flavored butter. Turn the chicken often and cook until the bird is mahogany brown and cooked through, about 30 minutes. Serve immediately.

Per Serving: 250 calories; 27 g. protein; 2 g. carbohydrate; 14 g. fat; 310 g. sodium; 104 mg. cholesterol.

Diana's Grilled Blackberry Chicken

Diana makes this chicken with split fryers or cornish hens. Either way, served on a bed of freshly picked blackberries and rice pilaf, it makes a midsummer dinner to remember.

serves 4
45 minutes, plus marinating overnight

1   **(3 to 4 pound) chicken, split down the back**
1   **pound blackberries, fresh or frozen**
1   **cup red wine vinegar**
½   **cup olive oil**
2   **bay leaves**
1   **teaspoon crushed thyme leaves**
        Salt to taste
        Pepper to taste

1. Flatten the split chicken by breaking the breast bone. Cover and refrigerate.
2. Reserve ¼ cup berries for garnish, then combine remaining berries with vinegar in a microwaveable dish, and raise to a boil in the microwave (about 1 minute on 100 percent [full] power). Remove and let the berries steep about an hour. Strain the berries, mashing them to remove the juice. Add olive oil, bay leaves, and thyme to juice. Divide the juice in half and refrigerate one part in a covered jar. Rub the remaining marinade into the bird, then recover and refrigerate overnight.
3. About 45 minutes before serving, preheat the grill. Remove the chicken from the refrigerator and discard the marinade in the dish. Pat the chicken dry and season to taste with salt and pepper. Grill until golden brown and done through, about 35 to 40 minutes, turning frequently and basting with the marinade saved in the jar.

Per Serving: 140 calories; 27 g. protein; 0 g. carbohydrate; 3 g. fat; 64 mg. sodium; 73 mg. cholesterol.

Pollo El Paso

Grill chicken breasts and serve on a bed of Southwestern vegetables for an easy, bright dinner.

serves 4
1 hour

4	**(4 ounce) boneless, skinless chicken breasts**
4	**tablespoons olive oil**
2	**tablespoons red wine vinegar**
1	**tablespoon honey**
½	**teaspoon chili powder**
	Salt
	Freshly ground black pepper
1	**(15 ounce) can black beans, rinsed and drained**
1	**cup whole corn kernels, cooked and drained**
½	**red onion, finely chopped**
1	**jalapeño pepper, seeded and minced**
½	**cup sliced black olives**
¼	**cup chopped fresh cilantro**
4	**tablespoons sour cream *or* plain nonfat yogurt**

1. Flatten chicken to ½ inch thickness between sheets of waxed paper and set aside.
2. Combine oil, vinegar, honey, and chili powder in a bowl. Reserve 2 tablespoons, then spoon remainder onto chicken. Cover and set aside.
3. Preheat grill.

4. While grill is preheating, combine beans, corn, onion, jalapeño pepper, black olives, and cilantro. Drizzle with reserved marinade. Adjust seasonings with salt and pepper.
5. Grill chicken meat until fork tender and golden brown on the outside, about 5 minutes per the side.
6. To serve, make a bed of combined vegetables and top with a smoking hot grilled chicken breast. Add a dollop of sour cream or plain yogurt. Serve with hot bread.

Per Serving: 435 calories; 32 g. protein; 27 g. carbohydrate; 22 g. fat; 151 mg. sodium; 73 mg. cholesterol.

The difference in fat and cholesterol is notable if you use yogurt instead of sour cream. You'll save 15 calories, 3 grams of fat, and 5 milligrams of cholesterol.

Chapter 4

REGIONAL FAVORITES

Chicken Palm Desert
Hawaiian Sweet and Sour Chicken
Carolina Barbecued Chicken
Jamaican Jerk Chicken
Hot Chicken Puffs
Country Captain
Chinatown Chicken Wings
Tex-Mex Chicken Molé
Mary Ann's Ohio Hunter's Chicken
Louisiana Chicken Sauce Piquant
Maryland Fried Chicken
Midwestern Jellied Chicken
Kassandra Vincent's Southern
Sweet Potato Chicken
Sherlyne Hutchinson's Citrus and
Red Onion Chicken

Chicken Palm Desert

This dish is fabulous served with couscous dappled with raisins, almonds, and chives. Kids especially like the mixture of chicken with black olives and sweet dates.

serves 4
1 hour, plus marinating overnight

4	chicken legs and thighs, separated
½	teaspoon ground cumin
½	teaspoon ground ginger
½	teaspoon salt
¼	teaspoon turmeric
1	teaspoon paprika
¼	teaspoon cinnamon
¼	teaspoon freshly ground black pepper
1	tablespoon olive oil
2	garlic cloves, smashed
1	cup mixed black and green olives
10	dates, pitted and halved
	Zest and juice from 1 lemon

1. Place chicken in a flat glass dish.

2. Combine spices and rub onto the chicken pieces. Cover and marinate overnight.

3. An hour before serving time, preheat a large skillet with oil and garlic, then add chicken pieces. Cover and cook over medium heat, turning frequently until the chicken is golden brown on all sides, about 20 minutes.

4. Sprinkle chicken with olives, dates, lemon zest, and juice. Add a teaspoon or so of water, cover, and continue cooking until thoroughly done, about 20 minutes. Serve hot or at room temperature.

Per Serving: 360 calories; 43 g. protein; 21 g. carbohydrate; 20 g. fat; 466 mg. sodium; 133 mg. cholesterol.

Hawaiian Sweet and Sour Chicken

Begin your own luau with a steaming platter of Hawaiian Sweet and Sour Chicken over rice with side dishes of coconut, crushed peanuts, scallions, pineapple cubes, macadamia nuts, and chopped red and green bell peppers.

serves 8
40 minutes

2½   **cups water**
¼   **cup cornstarch**
¾   **cup dark brown sugar**
1   **teaspoon salt**
1   **(20 ounce) can pineapple chunks, drained, reserving the juice**

2   **cups boneless, skinless chicken, light or dark, cut into chunks**
2   **tablespoons soy sauce**
¼   **cup rice vinegar**
2   **cups chicken stock (see page 24)**
2   **cups long grain rice**
1   **small onion, thinly sliced**
1   **green bell pepper, thinly sliced**
2   **large beefsteak tomatoes, cut in wedges**

1. In a large saucepan combine ½ cup water with cornstarch, brown sugar, and salt, and stir until smooth. Add reserved pineapple juice and cook over medium heat, stirring, until mixture begins to thicken, about 5 minutes.

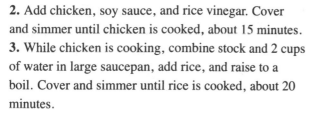

2. Add chicken, soy sauce, and rice vinegar. Cover and simmer until chicken is cooked, about 15 minutes.

3. While chicken is cooking, combine stock and 2 cups of water in large saucepan, add rice, and raise to a boil. Cover and simmer until rice is cooked, about 20 minutes.

4. Just before serving, add pineapple chunks, onion slices, and green pepper to chicken mixture. Cook and stir until vegetables begin to soften, no more than 3 minutes. Stir in tomato wedges.

5. Serve over hot cooked rice on a wide, flat platter. Place condiment dishes on the table for diners to add as they wish.

Per Serving: 361 calories; 14 g. protein; 68 g. carbohydrate; 3 g. fat; 493 mg. sodium; 29 mg. cholesterol.

Carolina Barbecued Chicken

What gets called barbecue depends on where you live. In the southeastern United States the term connotes vinegary, tart sauces and meat that's simmered in the oven.

serves 2
90 minutes, plus marinating overnight

1	**(3 to 4 pound) chicken, split down the back**
	Juice and zest of 1 lemon
¼	**cup cider vinegar**
¼	**cup water**
	Salt to taste
	Black pepper to taste
	Cayenne pepper to taste
4	**tablespoons butter**

1. Place chicken, skin side down, in a flat baking dish. Combine lemon juice and zest with vinegar and water and pour over the chicken. Cover and refrigerate overnight.

2. Season chicken to taste with salt, black pepper, and cayenne pepper. Add butter to the dish, then place in a 300°F oven and cook, uncovered, basting from time to time and turning after an hour so that the skin side is up. Cook until chicken is tender and golden brown, about 15 more minutes.

Per Serving: 280 calories; 54 g. protein; 0 g. carbohydrate; 6 mg. fat; 228 mg. sodium; 146 mg. cholesterol.

Jamaican Jerk Chicken

The Arawak Indians of Jamaica barbecued in a pit they called "jerk" and flavored their foods with native hot, sweet spices. Today, roadside barbecue stands offer exotic chicken, pork, or fish preparations drenched in Jamaican pimento (allspice) sauce. Marinate your bird overnight if you have the time, an hour or so if you just can't wait. Barbecue in a covered grill and you're coming close to authentic Jamaican jerk.

serves 6
1 hour, plus marinating overnight

1	tablespoon allspice berries
5	cloves garlic
	Knob of fresh ginger the size of your thumb
2	tablespoons dark brown sugar
1	teaspoon ground cinnamon
½	teaspoon dried thyme
1	small jalapeño pepper, seeded
2	scallions, green and white parts
½	teaspoon cayenne pepper
½	teaspoon finely ground black pepper
¼	teaspoon white pepper
½	teaspoon salt
½	cup olive oil
¼	cup red wine vinegar
	Juice and zest of 1 lime
12	pieces of chicken, your choice

1. Combine allspice, garlic, ginger, sugar, cinnamon, thyme, jalapeño pepper, scallion, cayenne, black, and white peppers, salt, oil, vinegar, and lime juice in a food processor or blender. Process until smooth.

2. Arrange chicken pieces in a large glass or plastic bowl. Rub on the marinade, lifting the skin of the pieces to rub it directly on the flesh. Cover and refrigerate until an hour before serving.

3. Preheat grill until coals are glowing white. Grill the chicken pieces, covered, turning several times, until the meat is thoroughly cooked, about 25 minutes.

Per Serving: 280 calories; 32 g. protein; 8 g. carbohydrate; 6 g. fat; 128 mg. sodium; 146 mg. cholesterol.

Hot Chicken Puffs

Terrific for lunch served in puff pastry shells, you can also offer this crunchy, hot chicken melange on a bed of butter lettuce. If you're using puff pastry, bake the shells while you're preparing the chicken and you'll save time.

serves 6
30 minutes

2   (4 ounce) boneless, skinless chicken breasts, poached
4   hard-boiled eggs, chopped
2   cups chopped celery
1   cup almonds
1   teaspoon butter
1   tablespoon minced onion
1   cup reduced calorie mayonnaise
    Juice and zest of ½ lemon
1   cup (4 ounces) low-fat cheddar cheese

1. Preheat the oven to 400°F.
2. Butter a 2-quart casserole dish. Micropoach chicken breasts by cooking with ½ cup water or broth, covered with plastic wrap in a microwave dish. Microwave at 100 percent (full) power for 8 minutes. Let chicken stand 5 minutes, then cut into bite-sized pieces.
3. In a medium bowl combine the cooked chicken, chopped eggs, and celery. Toss lightly and set aside.

4. In a small skillet, brown the almonds in butter then remove from heat and finely chop. Add to chicken mixture and toss.
5. In a small bowl combine the minced onion, mayonnaise, and lemon juice and zest; toss with chicken.
6. Place mixture in prepared dish, top with grated cheese and bake, uncovered, for 20 minutes.

Per Serving: 422 calories; 20 g. protein; 9 g. carbohydrate; 27 g. fat; 451 mg. sodium; 65 mg. cholesterol.

To reduce calories and fat, substitute plain yogurt for half the mayonnaise and reduce the cheese by half.

Country Captain

When Daisy Bonner cooked this old Georgia dish for President Franklin Roosevelt at his Warm Springs retreat, it soon became his favorite. This version varies from others in that the chicken is poached, not fried. Daisy Bonner always started with a good fat hen. If you can find one, you'll like the taste even better. Make a pot of rice to accompany this dish.

serves 6 to 8
2¹/₂ hours

1	(3 to 4 pound) hen or other chicken, cut into serving pieces
2	stalks celery
1	carrot
1	medium onion, quartered
2	medium onions, finely chopped
1	large green pepper, finely chopped
3	cloves garlic, minced
2	tablespoons margarine or butter
2	(16-ounce) cans tomatoes and juice
	Salt to taste
	Freshly ground black pepper to taste
1	teaspoon thyme
1	tablespoon curry powder
¹/₂	cup slivered blanched almonds, toasted
¹/₂	cup golden raisins

1. Poach chicken in barely salted water to cover with celery, carrot, and quartered onion until the meat falls from the bone, about 1¹/₂ hours. Skin and debone chicken. Place chicken pieces in an ovenproof casserole dish.

2. In a large skillet, sauté onions, green pepper, and garlic in margarine or butter. Add tomatoes and juice and cook 10 more minutes. Stir in salt and pepper along with thyme and curry powder. Cook 5 minutes. Pour the sauce over the chicken, cover and place in a 325°F oven and bake 45 minutes. Just before serving sprinkle the top with toasted almonds and raisins.

Per Serving: 255 calories; 31 g. protein; 10 g. carbohydrate; 10 g. fat; 718 mg. sodium; 75 mg. cholesterol.

To speed up this old-fashioned process, poach the chicken in the microwave. Place one cut-up chicken in a microwaveable baking dish, thick pieces to the outside of the dish. Add 2 stalks of celery, a cut-up carrot, and a cut-up onion. Add ³/₄ cup stock or water and salt to taste. Cover and cook at 100 percent (full) power for 22 minutes. Let the chicken stand 5 minutes before boning.

- Remember to strain and freeze the stock before using. It's so much better than store-bought chicken stock you'll wonder how you ever stood the canned stuff. Plus, you can control the salt.
- Taste the cooking water for salt. The saltier the water, the saltier the chicken will taste once it's poached.
- For a change, poach chicken in white wine, apple juice, or white grape juice.
- If you wish, fortify the stock with chicken bouillon.

Chinatown Chicken Wings

Here's an easy preparation that can fit any schedule. Serve on a bed of fluffy rice garnished with additional orange slices. It tastes even better reheated the next day.

serves 4
1 hour, plus marinating overnight

1½	**pounds chicken wings, without tips**
¼	**cup soy sauce**
1½	**teaspoons brown sugar**
¼	**teaspoon dry mustard**
2	**tablespoons peanut oil**
	Juice and zest of ½ orange
	Juice and zest of ½ lemon
	Fresh orange slices (garnish)

1. Arrange chicken wings one layer deep in a flat glass dish.
2. Combine soy sauce, sugar, mustard, oil, and citrus juices and zests. Pour the mixture over the chicken wings, then cover and refrigerate overnight.
3. In a 350°F oven, cook wings in the marinade, uncovered, until done, about 45 minutes. Turn occasionally. The chicken will have a delicious golden glaze and the marinade will have evaporated. During the last 2 to 3 minutes of cooking time, garnish the chicken with slices of fresh orange. Serve with rice and stir-fried vegetables.

Per Serving: 220 calories; 16 g. protein; 8 g. carbohydrate; 13 g. fat; 1015 mg. sodium; 146 mg. cholesterol.

You can cut the sodium by one third if you use low-sodium soy sauce.

Tex-Mex Chicken Molé

The original 21 herbs and spices chicken dish came from a Mexican nunnery where the nuns put their heads together to prepare a feast dish for a visiting bishop. Rich, hot, smoky, chocolate, and divine, it is our family's favorite way to finish off the Christmas turkey. Equally delicious with poached chicken, all you need to accompany it is a midwinter salad of grapefruit and avocado dotted with pomegranate seeds. It's a celebration feast.

serves 8
2 hours

1	(3 to 4 pound) chicken *or* 4 cups cooked chicken meat
1	(8¼ ounce) jar commercially prepared mole sauce
1	quart rich chicken stock (see page 24)
1	(7½ ounce) can tomato sauce
1	tablespoon smooth peanut butter
1	square unsweetened chocolate
1	tablespoon sugar
	Salt to taste
	Corn tortillas
	Slivered almonds (garnish)
	Sprigs of cilantro (garnish)

1. Stew a chicken in a pot just large enough to hold it, covered in water, until tender, about 1½ hours. Remove the chicken from the broth to cool. Strain both and reserve. Skin and debone the chicken and tear into bite-sized pieces. Cover and reserve. (This can be done the day before).

2. Warm the mole sauce in a large saucepot over low heat, until almost boiling. Stir in stock and simmer 20 minutes. Add tomato sauce, peanut butter, chocolate, and sugar. Cook and stir 20 more minutes. Salt to taste.

3. To serve, heat corn tortillas on a hot dry skillet about 15 seconds per side, then place one or two on a warmed plate. Spoon about ½ cup cooked chicken over the tortilla, and cover with sauce. Sprinkle with almonds and cilantro and serve. Alternately, you can place the mole and chicken over cooked long grain rice then garnish with almonds and cilantro.

Per Serving: 330 calories; 19 g. protein; 39 g. carbohydrate; 12 g. fat; 1009 mg. sodium; 89 mg. cholesterol.

Mary Ann's Ohio Hunter's Chicken

Originally, *cacciatore* meant "in the style of the hunter" to Italians; in other words, a field dinner made with the proceeds of the morning's hunt. Ohio hunters may do their hunting in the grocery store, but have refined this rustic one-pot dinner to suit the most discriminating diner. Be sure to pick up a loaf of French bread to mop up all the good juices.

serves 4
1 hour

1	(3 pound) frying chicken, cut into pieces
4	tablespoons olive oil
1	medium onion, coarsely chopped
1	green or yellow bell pepper, thinly sliced
4	cloves garlic, pressed
1	stalk of celery with leaves, chopped
1	tablespoon fresh rosemary needles *or* 1 teaspoon dried
	Pinch marjoram
	Salt to taste
	Freshly ground black pepper to taste
4	medium tomatoes, chopped
¼	cup chopped parsley
½	cup dry red wine
1	cup sliced fresh mushrooms (porcini mushrooms, if you can find them, are best here)

1. Wash and pat chicken pieces dry with a paper towel. Set aside. Heat oil over medium-high heat in a 12-inch skillet or roaster, then brown chicken pieces, a few at a time, until golden brown, about 15 minutes.

2. Meanwhile, cut the vegetables. When all the chicken pieces are browned, turn the heat down and add the onion, bell pepper, garlic, celery, and rosemary. Cook and stir until vegetables begin to brown, about 5 minutes. Season to taste with salt and pepper, then add tomatoes, parsley, and red wine. Cover and simmer until chicken is fork tender and juices run clear, about 30 minutes. Check from time to time and add more wine if necessary to keep the bird from becoming dry.

3. Add mushrooms, cover, and cook 10 more minutes.

4. Serve hot in wide-rimmed soup bowls with plenty of hot French bread.

Per Serving: 353 calories; 28 g. protein; 13 g. carbohydrate; 17 g. fat; 192 mg. sodium; 73 mg. cholesterol.

Louisiana Chicken Sauce Piquant

Generously season this dish with cayenne pepper and you'll see why the Cajuns call it piquant. If you don't own a black cast-iron pot to cook it in, try to borrow one. Unless some of the iron leaches out into the sauce, it just doesn't taste right. Be generous with the spices, and make a big pot of rice to cool the fires.

serves 8
1¹/₂ hours

1	cup vegetable oil
6	(6 ounce) bone-in chicken breasts
6	(10 ounces) bone-in chicken thigh and drumsticks

	Salt to taste
	Black pepper to taste
	White pepper to taste
	Cayenne pepper to taste
2	tablespoons unbleached white flour
4	large onions (about 3 pounds), finely chopped
6	cloves garlic, finely chopped
¹/₂	teaspoon dried thyme leaves
1	cup finely chopped celery with leaves
1	cup finely chopped green bell pepper
1	jalapeño pepper, seeded and minced (or to taste)
1	large tomato, minced
24	ounces tomato sauce
2	tablespoons Worcestershire sauce
¹/₂	teaspoon Tabasco sauce (or to taste)
2	cups chicken stock (see page 24)

1. Heat oil over medium-high heat in a large cast-iron pot until a drop of water leaps off.

2. Rub chicken pieces with salt, and black, white, and red peppers. Dust with flour, then brown, a few pieces at a time, in the oil. Remove chicken to paper towels.

3. Pour out all but 2 tablespoons of the oil then add onions, garlic, thyme, celery, and peppers. Cook and stir 10 to 15 minutes. Arrange chicken pieces on top of the vegetables.

4. Combine minced tomato, tomato sauce, Worcestershire sauce, Tabasco, and stock, then pour over the chicken. Lower heat and simmer slowly, uncovered, stirring from time to time until chicken is tender, about 45 minutes. Serve over long grain rice.

Per Serving: 383 calories; 35 g. protein; 11 g. carbohydrate; 22 g. fat; 372 mg. sodium; 87 mg. cholesterol.

Maryland Fried Chicken

The richness of this uptown fried chicken will make anybody throw over their fat-conscious diet at least for a day.

serves 6 to 8
1^1/$_2$ hours

2	**(3 to 4 pound) chickens, cut into serving pieces**
1	**cup unbleached white flour**
	Salt to taste
	Freshly ground black pepper to taste
2	**eggs, beaten slightly**
2	**cups plus 2 tablespoons half and half**
	Vegetable oil for frying
^{1}/$_4$	**cup hot tap water**
^{1}/$_4$	**cup butter**

1. Wash and dry chicken pieces.

2. Season flour with salt and pepper to taste.

3. Whisk eggs with 2 tablespoons half and half.

4. Dip each chicken piece into egg mixture, then into flour mixture, and set aside on wax paper. Reserve 2 tablespoons of seasoned flour for the gravy.

5. Pour vegetable oil into a 10-inch skillet until it is half filled. Heat over medium-high heat until water flicked into the hot oil jumps off. Brown the chicken pieces, a few at a time, turning the meat several times to equally brown all sides. Pour out all the oil. Place all chicken pieces back into the skillet, turn heat down to lowest setting, add ¼ cup hot tap water, then cover the skillet and let the chicken steam until done, about 30 minutes.

6. Once chicken is cooked, transfer it to a warm platter. Make gravy in the skillet by stirring the butter and reserved seasoned flour into the pan drippings. Cook and stir until golden then add 2 cups half and half, continuing to cook and stir until the mixture is thick and creamy.

7. If you wish, serve the chicken smothered under the gravy. Alternately, serve the gravy alongside the chicken.

Per Serving: 365 calories; 35 g. protein; 13 g. carbohydrate; 18 g. fat; 385 mg. sodium; 119 mg. cholesterol.

Midwestern Jellied Chicken

Carried forth from the time of the church supper, a cold chicken *en gelée* is low in calories, high in flavor, and lovely to look at. This recipe makes an extra cup of jelled broth so you can create those dazzling jewel squares to strew around the serving platter along with fresh herbs as garnish.

serves 6
3 days of cooking, cooling, and jelling

1	(3 to 4 pound) chicken
1	quart water
2	cups consommé
2	stalks celery, broken into pieces
1	carrot, broken
1	medium onion, studded with 4 cloves and halved
1	bay leaf
6	sprigs parsley
2	tablespoons fresh tarragon *or* 2 teaspoons dried
½	teaspoon white pepper
1	envelope unflavored gelatin
¼	cup cold water
	Juice and zest of ½ lemon
4	asparagus spears
6 to 8	thin red pepper strips
4	hard-cooked eggs, halved
	Fresh parsley (garnish)
	Fresh chives (garnish)
	Fresh tarragon (garnish)

Herb Mayonnaise

1	cup best quality mayonnaise
1	teaspoon capers
2	tablespoons each: fresh chopped parsley, chives, tarragon

1. Place chicken with water and consommé into a medium-sized stockpot. Add vegetables and seasonings. Raise to a boil over high heat, then reduce heat and simmer, uncovered, for 1 hour.

2. Remove chicken from broth, debone, and skin. Discard skin and bones and tear meat into bite-sized pieces. Generously oil a standard loaf pan, add chicken, cover, and refrigerate overnight.

3. Strain broth and refrigerate, covered, until the next day. Steam asparagus until al dente. Refrigerate. Hard-boil eggs and refrigerate.

4. The next day, remove all traces of fat from the top of the chilled broth then raise broth to a boil over high heat and reduce to 1½ cups. Soften gelatin in cold water and add to hot broth. Raise to a boil again, then add lemon juice and zest. Arrange cooked asparagus and red pepper strips over the chicken. Slowly pour the broth to ¾ inch of the top of the pan of chicken and refrigerate until beginning to firm, about 2 hours. The remaining hot broth should be poured into other oiled loaf pans, to a depth of ½ inch. Refrigerate loaf pans until they set.

5. When chicken is about half jelled in the clear, chilling broth, add shelled, halved hard-boiled eggs in the broth, cover, and refrigerate until completely chilled; overnight, if possible.

6. Just before serving, whisk capers and herbs into the mayonnaise. Unmold the chicken loaf by dipping the loaf pan into a pan of warm water, count to 30, then flip the loaf over a serving dish. The molded chicken should slip right out. Cut squares in the remaining gel, then sprinkle these jewels over the serving plate, around the molded chicken. Garnish with fresh herbs and serve alongside herbed mayonnaise.

Per Serving: 277 calories; 42 g. protein; 2 g. carbohydrate; 23 g. fat; 203 mg. sodium; 188 mg. cholesterol.

If you want crystal-clear gel, beat an egg white into the cold stock after you have thoroughly degreased the stock. Raise the broth to a simmer, stirring slowly with a slotted spoon. Egg whites will turn white and float to the top. Remove from the heat and slowly strain through a paper coffee filter. The stock will now be clear—just add softened gelatin.

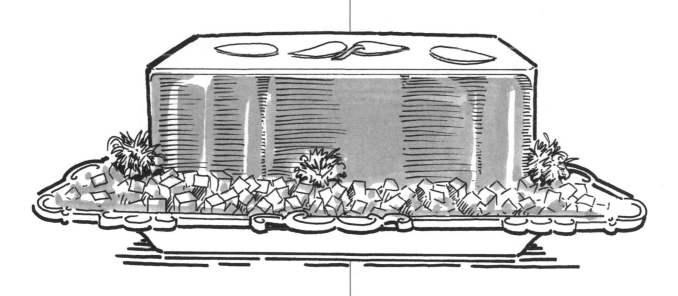

Kassandra Vincent's Southern Sweet Potato Chicken

National Chicken Cooking Contest Winner, Louisiana, 1991

Make a pan of corn bread, cook up some mustard greens, and you've got a Southern dinner deluxe.

serves 4
1 hour

4	**(4 ounce) boneless, skinless chicken breasts**
2	**tablespoons vegetable oil**
1	**cup evaporated milk**
2	**tablespoons honey**
1	**teaspoon salt**
¼	**teaspoon nutmeg**
¼	**teaspoon ground cloves**
1	**(16 ounce) can sweet potatoes, drained (reserve ¼ cup syrup)**
¼	**cup raisins**

1. Preheat the oven to 350°F.
2. Heat oil in a 10-inch skillet over medium-high heat, add chicken, and cook until lightly browned, about 10 minutes. Remove chicken pieces and drain. Place in a 13 × 9 × 2-inch baking dish.

3. In a small bowl, combine milk, honey, salt, nutmeg, and cloves. Pour over the chicken. Bake in preheated oven, uncovered, for 10 minutes.
4. Arrange sweet potatoes and raisins around the chicken pieces. Pour reserved syrup over the dish and return to the oven. Cook until chicken is fork tender, about 30 to 40 minutes.

Per Serving: 365 calories; 32 g. protein; 27 g. carbohydrate; 15 g. fat; 789 mg. sodium; 92 mg. cholesterol.

Sherlyne Hutchinson's Citrus and Oregon Red Onion Chicken

National Chicken Cooking Contest Winner, Oregon, 1991

Serve this zesty chicken entree with red pepper spiked polenta, steamed broccoli, and crusty French bread.

serves 6
45 minutes, plus marinating an hour

6	**(4 ounce) boneless, skinless chicken breasts**
¼	**cup frozen orange juice concentrate**
	Juice and zest of half a lemon
	Juice and zest of half a lime
1	**teaspoon granulated chicken bouillion**
2	**tablespoons minced fresh cilantro**
⅓	**cup flour**
1½	**tablespoons butter**

Red Onion Relish

1½	**cups diced red onion**
1½	**tablespoons butter**
1½	**tablespoons sugar**
3	**tablespoons red wine vinegar**
1	**tablespoon water**
1	**teaspoon anise seed**

1. Flatten chicken breasts between sheets of waxed paper to ½ inch thickness. In a medium bowl mix orange, lemon, and lime juices. Stir in bouillion and cilantro. Add chicken, turning to coat. Cover and refrigerate 1 hour.

2. Meanwhile, prepare red onion relish by combining diced red onion, butter and sugar in a saucepan. Cook over medium heat, stirring, until onion is translucent, about 10 minutes. Add vinegar and water, cook, stirring occasionally, 3 more minutes. Remove from the heat and add anise seed. Set aside.

3. Remove chicken from the marinade and drain. Reserve marinade. Dredge chicken in flour and set aside.

4. Heat butter in a 10-inch skillet then sauté the breasts, browning on all sides. Add reserved marinade, reduce heat, and cook 10 minutes or until liquid is reduced and the meat is fork tender. (It is important to cook marinade thoroughly to make sure microbes from raw chicken have been killed.)

5. To serve, place the chicken on a platter, sprinkle with citrus zest and trail a heaping spoonful of red onion relish from the center to the side of each piece.

Per Serving: 380 calories; 31 g. protein; 17 g. carbohydrate; 4 g. fat; 520 mg. sodium; 100 mg. cholesterol.

Chapter 5

ONE-DISH DINNERS, CASSEROLES, PIES, AND STEWS

Chicken Vindaloo
Chicken Thyme Stew
Chicken à la King
Chicken Paella
Chicken Pot-Au-Feu
Chicken Tetrazzini
Chicken Bon Femme
Chicken Comfort
Chicken Easy
Chinese Chicken Noodle
Carol Skinner's Pollo Sabroso
Maureen Gestwicki's Hungarian
Baked Chicken
Beggar's Chicken
Deep-Dish Chicken Pie with Low-Fat
Tarragon Biscuits
White Chicken Chili
Chicken Zuke Bake

Chicken Vindaloo

Cook 1 cup of basmati rice in 2 cups of water for 20 minutes covered, and you're set for a one-dish dinner that is flavored with peppers and mustard, brightly colored with the saffron yellow of turmeric, the brilliant red of tomatoes, and the dazzling green of cilantro. This dinner is almost too good to waste on a weeknight dinner, but it's so easy, how can you resist? Although it's best if you refrigerate the marinated chicken overnight, you can cook it with good results after only an hour of marinating, covered, on the counter.

serves 4 to 6
1 hour, plus marinating overnight

1	(3 to 4 pound) chicken, quartered and skinned
¼	cup rice wine vinegar
2	tablespoons molasses
2	teaspoons ground turmeric
2	teaspoons whole coriander seeds
1	teaspoon whole cumin seeds
1	tablespoon chili powder
1	teaspoon dry mustard
½	teaspoon salt
2	cloves garlic, finely chopped
2	fresh jalapeño peppers, seeded and finely chopped
2	tablespoons olive oil

1	large onion, finely sliced
3	medium tomatoes, quartered
8	small new potatoes, boiled and halved
	Fresh cilantro (garnish)

1. Place chicken in a glass dish, skin side down. In another bowl mix the vinegar, molasses, turmeric, coriander, cumin, chili powder, mustard, salt, garlic, and jalapeño peppers. Pour over the chicken. Cover and marinate overnight in the refrigerator.

2. Forty-five minutes before serving time, start a pot of rice, then heat oil in a 10-inch skillet over medium-high heat. Sauté the onion slices until limp and beginning to turn golden brown, about 5 minutes. Remove the onion and brown the chicken pieces in the hot oil until golden brown all over, about 5 minutes. Reduce the heat, add onion to the chicken, arrange the tomato wedges and cooked new potatoes around the chicken, pour on the reserved marinade, cover, and cook until the chicken is fork tender and the leg joint moves freely, about 20 minutes.

3. To serve, arrange a scoop of cooked rice on the plate and top with a piece of chicken, some potatoes, and tomato wedges. Drizzle some of the hot, thin sauce over, decorate with cilantro, and take a deep whiff of that lovely aroma.

Per Serving: 590 calories; 46 g. protein; 27 g. carbohydrate; 30 g. fat; 180 mg. sodium; 175 mg. cholesterol.

Chicken Thyme Stew

The French have long known that chicken and thyme are a flavor marriage made in heaven. The modern treatment of this dish begins with chunks of chicken thigh and breast meat, allowing the flavors to come together faster. Leave the stew to simmer slowly while you relax. A great choice for company on a night when stew, crusty French bread, and salad is all you'll want; and maybe a glass of wine, and a fire, and great friends.

serves 8
approximately 1 hour

4	tablespoons olive oil
2	(4 ounce) boneless, skinless chicken breasts, cut into chunks
3	(5 ounce) boneless, skinless chicken thighs, cut into chunks
8	medium (2 pounds) red potatoes, quartered
4	medium carrots, (1 pound) scraped, and sliced into 1/2-inch-long pieces
1	large yellow onion (1/2 pound), peeled and coarsely chopped
6	cloves garlic, peeled and finely chopped
1/2	teaspoon sugar
	Salt to taste
	Freshly ground black pepper to taste
2	tablespoons unbleached white flour

4   cups chicken stock (see page 24)
1   cup dry red wine, preferably burgundy
2   tablespoons fresh thyme leaves *or*
    1½ teaspoons dried
1   teaspoon cracked black peppercorns
½   pound fresh mushrooms, coarsely chopped
1   cup finely chopped fresh parsley leaves

1. In a large stockpot heat olive oil over medium-high heat until it sizzles. One ingredient at a time, add the chicken chunks, potatoes, carrots, onion, and garlic. Season with sugar, salt, and pepper. Cook, stirring occasionally, until chicken is no longer pink, about 20 minutes.

2. Sprinkle flour over the mixture and cook, stirring 2 more minutes. Pour in chicken broth, wine, and thyme. Raise to a boil, then add mushrooms. Reduce heat and simmer until vegetables are tender, about 20 minutes. Stir in parsley, season to taste with salt and pepper, then serve in wide-rimmed soup bowls.

Per Serving: 332 calories; 27 g. protein; 45 g. carbohydrate; 27 g. fat; 505 mg. sodium; 8 g. cholesterol.

To slash the salt in this healthy, delicious stew, use homemade chicken broth; even "reduced-salt" commercial stock has more sodium than your own homemade version (see page 24).

Chicken à la King

We've lightened this American classic by using a glazing of olive oil instead of a plug of butter and by removing all the skin and fat from the chicken before stirring it into the flavor-drenched sauce. Even with the fats and calories reduced by 25 percent, this is still a favorite.

serves 4
1 hour

8   boned, skinned chicken thighs
4   tablespoons olive oil
1   cup mushrooms, sliced
1   small red bell pepper, seeded and chopped
1   cup sugar snap peas
1   carrot, peeled and sliced
¼   cup unbleached white flour
2   cups chicken stock (see page 24)
    Salt to taste
    Freshly ground black pepper to taste
    Thick slices of whole wheat bread
2   tablespoons snipped chives

1. In a 10-inch skillet, sauté the chicken thighs in 1 tablespoon of oil until brown and done, about 20 minutes, turning from time to time. Remove thighs and cut into bite-sized pieces.

2. Add 1 more tablespoon oil to the skillet and sauté mushrooms and bell pepper until limp and clear, about 5 minutes.

3. Meanwhile, bring a medium-sized pot of water to a boil. Place peas in a steamer and lower into the water. Cook one minute, then lift the steamer from the boiling water. Refresh under cold running water to stop them from cooking. Repeat this process with the carrots.

4. Sprinkle flour over the mushrooms and bell pepper and add remaining 2 tablespoons oil. Cook and stir about 3 minutes, then stir in the broth, whisking until free of lumps. Cook until the mixture is thick, and season to taste with salt and pepper.

5. Stir in the cooked chicken, peas, and carrots. Bring to a simmer and cook about 10 minutes.

6. Meanwhile, toast the bread and arrange on dinner plates. Spoon chicken and sauce over the toast and sprinkle with chives. Serve immediately.

Per Serving: 340 calories; 27 g. protein; 12 g. carbohydrate; 28 g. fat; 660 mg. sodium; 121 mg. cholesterol.

Chicken Paella

This Spanish peasant dish made use of whatever foods could be hunted or gathered then thrown into the pan. The dish is named after the pan it's cooked in, and the paella pan looks a lot like the one goldminers used to pan for gold. If you have a deep-sided chicken frying skillet, that's a close approximation of the paella pan. If not, use a fireproof casserole, at least 12 inches in diameter with 1½-inch-high sides.

If you'd like to enjoy this dish the way the Spaniards meant it to be enjoyed, cook the whole thing outdoors over an open fire. Ad-lib the meats and fishes to suit, adding or subtracting as it pleases you.

serves 4
1 hour

1	**pound boneless, skinless chicken thighs**
½	**pound boneless ham**
8	**shrimp**
12	**clams and/or mussels**
¼	**cup olive oil**
1	**large yellow onion, chopped**
4	**cloves garlic, minced**
1	**green bell pepper, cut in strips**
1	**red bell pepper, cut in strips**
1	**cup chicken stock (see page 24)**
1	**cup dry white wine**
2	**medium tomatoes, chopped**

2   tablespoons tomato paste
1   bay leaf
1   tablespoon fresh thyme *or* 1 teaspoon dried
1½   teaspoons paprika
1½   cups arborio or other short-grained rice
       Pinch saffron threads
       Salt to taste
       Pepper to taste
1   cup peas, fresh or frozen

1. Cut chicken and ham into bite-sized pieces then set aside. Cook seafood in 1 cup boiling water until shrimp turns pink, about 3 minutes. Remove from the heat and reserve.

2. Heat olive oil in the paella pan, then fry chicken and ham until done. Remove meat from the pan and reserve. Add onion and garlic to the pan and cook until onion turns clear, about 5 minutes. Add peppers and continue cooking and stirring until peppers brown, about 5 minutes more.

3. Meanwhile, lift seafood from the other saucepan, and combine seafood broth with chicken stock and white wine; raise to a boil.

4. Add the tomatoes, tomato paste, bay leaf, thyme, and paprika to the paella pan. Cook about 5 minutes, then stir in rice and saffron; stir fry about 5 minutes. Pour in boiling broth. Cook and stir over high heat about 5 more minutes, then reduce heat, season to taste with salt and pepper, and continue cooking, uncovered, until rice is done and liquid is absorbed, about 15 minutes. Stir in peas, meat, and seafood, cover, and let stand at reduced heat 5 minutes before serving.

Per Serving: 325 calories; 31 g. protein; 10 g. carbohydrate; 10 g. fat; 435 mg. sodium; 91 mg. cholesterol.

Chicken Pot-Au-Feu

Yes, yes, I know this takes two days to make. But it doesn't require much effort, only a good bit of time. Trust me, it's worth it—rich chicken broth with fallen-from-the-bone chicken and good winter vegetables. All you need to make a comforting midwinter dinner is a loaf of black bread.

serves 4
1 hour, plus cooling overnight

1	(3 pound) chicken, quartered, with giblets
1	quart of water
1	onion
2	ribs celery
1	carrot, sliced
2	tablespoons granulated chicken bouillon
3	sprigs parsley
1	teaspoon salt

Pot-au-feu

	Reserved chicken broth
1	head cabbage, cut into 8 pieces
16	pearl onions, peeled
4	carrots, pared and sliced
2	ribs celery, sliced
1	cup green peas, fresh or frozen
	Salt to taste
	Pepper to taste

1. Place chicken and giblets in a 5-quart dutch oven. Add water and remaining ingredients. Raise to a boil, cover, and reduce heat. Simmer 40 minutes or until chicken is tender. Remove from the heat and strain the broth.
2. Refrigerate the chicken in the strained broth overnight, then skim and discard chicken fat from the broth.
3. Lift the chicken from the broth, debone, skin, and cut into bite-sized pieces.
4. Forty-five minutes before serving, heat the broth in a large saucepot. Add cabbage and onions and boil until vegetables are tender, about 20 minutes. Add carrots and celery and boil 10 more minutes. Add peas and chicken, cover, and cook 5 more minutes. Adjust seasonings with salt and pepper.
5. Serve in wide-rimmed soup bowls.

Per Serving: 215 calories; 22 g. protein; 20 g. carbohydrate; 5 g. fat; 177 mg. sodium; 58 mg. cholesterol.

Chicken Tetrazzini

Serve this favorite American-Italian dinner with spaghetti. Begin the meal with traditional Italian antipasti—carrots, celery, pickled peppers—then serve the main course with crusty French bread.

serves 4
45 minutes

3	tablespoons olive oil
2	cups thinly sliced fresh mushrooms
1	medium onion, coarsely chopped
3	tablespoons unbleached white flour
1	pint chicken stock (see page 24)
1/2	cup half and half
	Salt to taste
	Cayenne pepper to taste
	Black pepper to taste
1/4	teaspoon ground nutmeg
1	bay leaf
2	whole cloves
3/4	pound boneless, skinless chicken thigh meat, cut into 1/2-inch strips
	Parmesan cheese
	Italian parsley sprigs (garnish)

1. Make a big pot of spaghetti according to package directions.
2. Meanwhile, place a 10-inch skillet over medium-high heat, add 1 tablespoon oil, and heat.
3. Sauté mushrooms in oil until tender and beginning to soften, about 5 minutes. Transfer to a warm bowl and reserve.
4. Heat another tablespoon of oil in the skillet then sauté onion, just until translucent and tender, about 3 minutes.
5. Sprinkle flour over the onions and cook and stir for 2 more minutes. Stir in broth, half and half, salt, cayenne pepper, black pepper, nutmeg, bay leaf, and cloves. Raise to a boil and cook for 2 to 3 minutes.
6. Add chicken to boiling broth and cook until no longer pink, about 4 minutes. Add reserved mushrooms and cook another minute or so.
7. To serve, mound cooked spaghetti on a plate, then top with chicken. Sprinkle with parmesan cheese and garnish with a sprig of Italian parsley.

Per Serving: 568 calories; 43 g. protein; 54 g. carbohydrate; 20 g. fat; 865 mg. sodium; 117 mg. cholesterol.

Chicken Bon Femme

Count on the French to take a dish as simple as pot roast, substitute a chicken, and come up with a dish so delectable they named it for the good lady who figured it out.

serves 4 to 6
2 hours

4	**tablespoons butter or margarine, softened**
2	**cloves garlic, minced**
1	**teaspoon fresh thyme leaves** *or* **¹⁄₂ teaspoon dried**
	Juice of ¹⁄₂ lemon
¹⁄₄	**pound bacon**
1	**3 pound chicken**
3	**medium carrots, peeled and chunked**
4	**medium russet potatoes, peeled and chunked**
2	**medium yellow onions, peeled and thinly sliced**
	Salt to taste
	Pepper to taste
	Chopped parsley (garnish)

1. Preheat the oven to 350°F.
2. Mash together butter, garlic, thyme, and lemon juice. Rub half this paste into chicken cavity, and reserve the rest.
3. Fry bacon in a chicken roaster until crisp, then remove the bacon and brown the chicken in the hot fat until golden on all sides.

4. While the chicken is browning, heat reserved butter mixture in a skillet and sauté carrots, potatoes, and onions until golden brown, about 10 minutes.
5. Once chicken is browned, remove it from the roaster and drain any remaining fat. Place the chicken back in the roaster, crumble the bacon over it, and add the browned vegetables. Season to taste with salt and pepper.
6. Cover and bake in the preheated oven until done, about 90 minutes. The juices should run clear and the leg joint will move freely. Sprinkle with parsley just before serving.

Per Serving: 369 calories; 30 g. protein; 23 g. carbohydrate; 16 g. fat; 317 mg. sodium; 108 mg. cholesterol.

Chicken Comfort

The comforting aspect of this recipe is that it makes use of any half cup of jelly you find languishing in your refrigerator. The original recipe used plum, but I've had equally good results with apricot, orange marmalade, and crab apple. The glaze is what you're after. And is this easy? Yes, yes.

serves 4
20 minutes

4 (4 ounce) boneless, skinless chicken breasts
½ small onion, minced
   Thumb-sized piece of fresh ginger, grated
1 tablespoon vegetable oil
1 tablespoon soy sauce
1 teaspoon Dijon mustard
   Juice and pulp of 1 seeded orange
½ cup jelly (plum, apricot—whatever is available)

1. Preheat the oven to 475°F.
2. Tear chicken into bite-sized chunks.
3. Make the sauce by combining the remaining ingredients. Place chicken in a flat glass dish. Rub the sauce into the chicken pieces and let it stand, covered, while the oven preheats. Bake, uncovered, until the chicken is a lovely golden-brown, about 10 minutes.
4. Serve alongside angel hair pasta with some steamed broccoli.

Per Serving: 302 calories; 27 g. protein; 33 g. carbohydrate; 7 g. fat; 363 mg. sodium; 73 mg. cholesterol.

Chicken Easy

Don't you love recipes that go together and into the oven with almost no intermediate steps? This bird comes out golden, pungent, and begging for a bed of noodles.

serves 4
1 hour

8 (1½ pounds) boneless, skinless chicken thighs
   Freshly ground black pepper to taste
   Cayenne pepper to taste
   Salt to taste
1 tablespoon butter or margarine
1 (6 ounce) can frozen orange juice concentrate
1 (6 ounce) can broth (or see page 24)
½ cup toasted slivered almonds

1. Preheat the oven to 350°F.
2. Arrange chicken pieces in a shallow baking pan. Season generously with peppers and salt lightly.
3. In a microwaveable bowl, combine butter, juice concentrate, and broth. Raise to a boil at 100 percent (full) power, about 3 minutes, then pour over the chicken.
4. Bake, uncovered, until tender and golden, about 45 minutes, basting and turning thighs from time to time.
5. To serve, sprinkle with toasted, slivered almonds.

Per Serving: 312 calories; 26 g. protein; 23 g. carbohydrate; 12 g. fat; 340 mg. sodium; 82 mg. cholesterol.

Chinese Chicken Noodle

Serve this one-dish dinner in a soup bowl the way the Chinese do, sometimes known as a dry soup. In other words, most of the broth is absorbed by the vegetables and noodles, offering you a flavor-drenched, soft noodle dinner. If you don't have all these vegetables on hand, substitute, adding more of another until you have a total of 3½ cups.

serves 4
30 minutes

2   (4 ounce) boneless, skinless chicken breasts, cut into 1-inch strips
1   cup fresh broccoli florets, divided into bite-sized pieces
½   cup red bell pepper, julienned
1   cup julienned carrots
½   cup fresh mushrooms, cut into bite-sized pieces
½   cup jicama or water chestnuts, cut into bite-sized pieces
1   tablespoon peanut (or other vegetable) oil
1   tablespoon grated fresh ginger
2   cloves garlic, pressed
2   scallions, green and white parts, cut into 1-inch pieces
1½ cups chicken stock (see page 24)
1   tablespoon soy sauce
½   teaspoon sugar
4   ounces uncooked angel hair pasta *or* vermicelli
2   teaspoons cornstarch
2   tablespoons water
    Salt to taste
    Pepper to taste
    Toasted sesame seeds

1. Soak cut vegetables in a bowl of ice water before cooking.

2. Heat oil in a wok over medium-high heat. Fry ginger, garlic, and scallions until beginning to brown, less than 1 minute. Add chicken strips and stir fry until chicken is beginning to brown and is opaque-white throughout, about 5 minutes.

3. Pour in chicken broth and soy sauce, then sprinkle with sugar. Raise to a boil.

4. Meanwhile, drain the vegetables and add to the wok. Stir in pasta, reduce heat, cover, and simmer until the pasta is al dente, about 5 to 8 minutes.

5. While the pasta is cooking, combine the cornstarch and water in a small bowl. Stir into the mixture in the work, cook until thickened, about 1 minute, stirring constantly. Season to taste with salt and pepper.

6. Divide among 4 soup bowls, sprinkle with toasted sesame seeds, and serve immediately.

Per Serving: 310 calories; 34 g. protein; 33 g. carbohydrate; 5 g. fat; 840 mg. sodium; 71 mg. cholesterol.

This dish is delicious made with rice vermicelli as well. Remember to soak the threads in cool water 2 minutes, then drain before cooking. Rice vermicelli and toasted sesame seeds are found in Asian markets and the oriental section of many supermarkets.

Carol Skinner's Pollo Sabroso

National Chicken Cooking Contest Winner, Colorado, 1991

Make a pot of yellow rice, some guacamole, an icy Mexican beer, and tortilla chips and it's a Southwestern dinner supreme.

serves 4
1 hour

4	(4 ounce) boneless, skinless chicken breasts
1	tablespoon plus 2 teaspoons olive oil
	Juice of 1 lemon
	Salt to taste
	Pepper to taste
1	medium yellow onion, finely chopped
2	large garlic cloves, minced
1	tablespoon chili powder
1/4	teaspoon ground cloves
1/4	teaspoon ground cumin
1/4	teaspoon coriander
3	cups roughly chopped tomatoes and juice
2	tablespoons honey
1	cup pitted, chopped black olives
	Chopped fresh parsley or cilantro (garnish)

1. Preheat oven to 350°F.

2. Coat a baking dish lightly with 1 tablespoon oil. Place chicken in baking dish with half the lemon juice, then season to taste with salt and pepper. Cover and refrigerate.

3. Heat remaining 2 teaspoons oil in a 10-inch skillet over medium heat. Add onion, garlic, chili powder, cloves, cumin, and coriander. Cook and stir until onion is translucent, about 10 minutes. Add tomatoes and juice, honey, olives, and remaining lemon juice. Simmer 20 minutes. Season to taste with salt and pepper. Pour sauce over the chicken.

4. Bake chicken in preheated oven, uncovered, until meat is fork tender, about 30 minutes. Garnish with chopped cilantro or parsley.

Per Serving: 363 calories; 28 g. protein; 12 g. carbohydrate; 21 g. fat; 395 mg. sodium; 73 mg. cholesterol.

Maureen Gestwicki's Hungarian Baked Chicken

National Chicken Cooking Contest Winner, West Virginia, 1991

This is a classic brought over from the old country that has withstood the test of time. Serve with a side of buttered noodles and dark rye bread.

serves 4
1 hour

8	chicken legs *or* 4 leg-thigh pieces
1	teaspoon Hungarian paprika
1	teaspoon salt
½	teaspoon pepper
¼	cup margarine
1	small head cabbage, cored and cut into ½-inch wedges
2	red cooking apples, cored and thinly sliced
1	medium onion, thinly sliced
2	tablespoons grated lemon zest
1	tablespoon caraway seed
2	teaspoons sugar
1½	cups shredded Swiss cheese
1	piece bacon, fried crisp and crumbled
	Parsley (garnish)
	Radishes (garnish)

1. Preheat the oven to 375°F.

2. Sprinkle chicken with paprika, half the salt, half the pepper, and set aside.

3. Heat 2 tablespoons margarine in a 10-inch skillet and brown chicken pieces until golden on all sides, about 10 minutes.

4. Meanwhile, grease the bottom of a 9-inch deep-dish pie plate with all but 1 tablespoon margarine. Add cabbage and dot with remaining margarine. Sprinkle with remaining salt and pepper. Cover and bake in preheated oven until tender-crisp, about 20 minutes.

5. Uncover and place apples and onion over the cabbage. Sprinkle with lemon zest, caraway seeds, and sugar. Place browned chicken pieces on top, cover, and bake until chicken is fork tender, about 30 minutes.

6. To serve, remove from the oven and sprinkle with grated cheese and crumbled bacon. Garnish with parsley and radishes and serve immediately.

Per Serving: 345 calories; 35 g. protein; 19 g. carbohydrate; 13 g. fat; 237 mg. sodium; 111 mg. cholesterol.

Beggar's Chicken

Originally, so the story goes, a beggar stole a chicken, plucked it, wrapped it in leaves, then—for want of a pot—coated the wrapped bird in mud, buried it in the ground with some live coals, and went away. When he returned a few hours later, his feast was ready.

Today, for want of a firepit, you can place the chicken in cabbage leaves in a deep, ovenproof casserole dish, seal the edges with a flour and water paste, and bake in a slow oven. Once you crack open the sealed casserole, take a deep whiff of that aroma. Ah, the life of the beggar.

serves 4
2¹/₄ hours

1	**(3 to 4 pound) chicken**
	Salt to taste
	Freshly ground black pepper to taste
1	**tablespoon oil**
6	**outer leaves of a cabbage**
3	**celery ribs, broken into pieces**
1	**medium onion, cut into thick slices**
1	**head of garlic, divided into cloves but not peeled**

Bouquet Garni

6   sprigs parsley
2   sprigs rosemary
4   sage leaves
2   sprigs thyme
1   bay leaf

Beggar's Paste

1   cup unbleached white flour
1   tablespoon salt
     Water to moisten to a thick paste

1. Preheat oven to 325°F.
2. Add oil to a 10-inch skillet and heat over medium-high heat. Season a whole chicken to taste with salt and pepper, then brown, about 20 minutes.
3. Meanwhile, line a large, deep, 4-quart ovenproof casserole dish with all but one of the cabbage leaves. Lay the celery and onion slices on the bottom of the dish on top of the cabbage leaves.
4. Once chicken is browned, lay on the cabbage-onion-celery bed. Toss garlic in the hot skillet until you smell the garlic and the cloves are beginning to brown, about 2 minutes. Add the garlic to the chicken.
5. Combine *bouquet garni* herbs in a piece of cheese-cloth and tie with a string. Place the herbs in the cavity of the bird, then place the last piece of cabbage on top.
6. Make the flour and water paste. It should be about the consistency of grade school glue. Cover the casserole dish with a lid, then seal the lid closed with the paste. Bake in preheated oven for 1½ hours.

7. Remove the casserole from the oven and let stand 10 minutes before breaking the seal around the lid, To open, insert a sharp knife under the dried paste. Remove and discard bouquet garni and serve immediately. Spoon the pan juices over rice or mashed potatoes if desired.

Per Serving: 250 calories; 38 g. protein; 12 g. carbohydrate; 13 g. fat; 220 mg. sodium; 116 mg. cholesterol.

Deep-Dish Chicken Pie with Low-Fat Tarragon Biscuits

Poach the chicken, make some low-fat yeast biscuits, and you'll soon have an aromatic, one-dish chicken dinner.

serves 6
90 minutes

Biscuits

2	cups unbleached white flour
1	teaspoon baking powder
1	teaspoon salt
1	teaspoon dried thyme
1	teaspoon dried tarragon
2	tablespoons vegetable shortening
1	tablespoon sugar
1	tablespoon 50 percent faster dry active yeast
2	tablespoons water, or as needed
²/₃	cup low-fat buttermilk, heated to lukewarm

Chicken Filling

6	chicken thighs
1	tablespoon olive oil
1	leek, with 1-inch of green, cut in half, washed thoroughly to remove sand
1	carrot, chopped
1/4	pound mushrooms, quartered
1	teaspoon Worcestershire sauce
1	teaspoon dried thyme
1	teaspoon lemon zest
1	cup chicken stock
1	tablespoon cornstarch dissolved in 2 tablespoons water
1/2	cup peas, fresh or frozen, thawed
	Salt to taste
	Freshly ground black pepper to taste

1. To make the biscuits combine flour, baking powder, salt, and herbs in a medium-sized bowl and stir to mix. Cut in shortening (this is easy to do in a food processor) until mixture resembles coarse meal.

2. Stir sugar, yeast, and water into the warmed buttermilk, then pour into the flour mixture. Stir until mixture forms a loose ball.

3. Pat into a 1/2-inch-thick circle. Cut out biscuits with 1 1/2-inch cutter and place on a flour-dusted piece of wax paper in a warm, draft-free place to rise until almost doubled in bulk, about 20 minutes.

4. While the dough is rising, poach chicken pieces in simmering water to cover for 20 minutes. Turn off the heat and let the chicken cool in the broth, then debone and skin chicken, cut into bite-sized pieces, and reserve broth.

5. While biscuits rise and chicken cooks, preheat the oven to 400°F. Begin cooking vegetables by heating oil in a 10-inch skillet. When hot, add leeks, carrot, and mushrooms, and sauté until soft and beginning to brown on the edges, about 10 minutes.

6. Stir in Worcestershire, thyme, lemon zest, and reserved chicken stock. Add cornstarch dissolved in water and cook and stir until thickened. Remove from the heat and stir in the chicken and peas. Season to taste with salt and pepper. Pour mixture into a 9-inch deep-dish pie plate or quiche dish.

7. Carefully transfer raised biscuits to the top of the chicken filling then bake in preheated oven until the biscuits are browned, about 20 minutes.

Per Serving: 340 calories; 43 g. protein; 63 g. carbohydrate; 16 g. fat; 695 mg. sodium; 76 mg. cholesterol.

White Chicken Chili

For a zesty change from beef chili, make this glorious, healthful lentil and chicken chili. Serve with a side of homebaked tortilla chips and you have an almost fat-free dinner.

serves 6
1 hour

6	**(4 ounce) boneless, skinless chicken breasts**
1	**cup lentils**
2	**cups chicken stock (see page 24)**
2	**tablespoons olive oil**
1	**medium onion, finely chopped**
2	**cloves garlic, minced**
½	**medium green bell pepper, finely chopped**
½	**medium red bell pepper, finely chopped**
1	**tablespoon chili powder**
½	**teaspoon cumin**
½	**teaspoon oregano leaves**
1	**(4 ounce) can diced green chilis**
1	**(1¾ pound) can crushed stewed tomatoes**
½	**cup shredded white cheddar cheese**
½	**red pepper, cut into rings**
½	**green pepper, cut into strips**
	Dollop of plain nonfat yogurt
	Whole black olives

1. Cut chicken into bite-sized pieces and set aside.

2. Place lentils and chicken broth in a stockpot. Raise to a boil over high heat then reduce to a simmer, cover, and cook 30 minutes.

3. Meanwhile, in a 10-inch skillet, heat oil then add chicken pieces and cook, stirring constantly, until chicken becomes opaque, about 4 minutes. Remove chicken and reserve.

4. Sauté onion, garlic, and peppers with chili powder, cumin, and oregano until they begin to brown, about 10 minutes. Add green chilis, tomatoes, and chicken, cover, and simmer until lentils are done.

5. Pour cooked vegetables and chicken into cooked lentils, season to taste with salt and pepper, and simmer an additional 30 minutes.

6. Serve from a tureen and add grated cheddar and pepper rings for garnish. Top with a dollop of plain yogurt and whole black olives.

Per Serving: 295 calories; 32 g. protein; 21 g. carbohydrate; 6 g. fat; 266 mg. sodium; 73 mg. cholesterol.

Chicken Zuke Bake

When your garden is overflowing with zucchini and you'd rather lie about than cook, this supper bakes while you work on your tan. Serve with crusty French bread, a tossed salad, and a pitcher of cold lemonade.

serves 4
1 hour

1	cup plain bread crumbs
1	large egg
1	tablespoon water
	Grating of fresh black pepper
4	(4 ounce) boneless, skinless chicken breast halves
¼	cup olive oil
2	large zucchini, cut into thick diagonal slices
2	large tomatoes, thinly sliced
¼	cup fresh basil leaves, crushed
4	ounces part-skim mozzarella cheese, shredded
½	cup grated parmesan cheese

1. Preheat oven to 400°F.
2. Arrange bread crumbs on a piece of wax paper. In a pie plate whisk together the egg, water, and pepper. Dip zucchini slices into egg mixture then coat with bread crumbs. Set aside. Repeat this process with the chicken; dip into egg mixture than coat with bread crumbs. Set aside.
3. Preheat a 10-inch skillet over medium-high heat. Add 1 tablespoon or so of oil to coat the bottom of the skillet, then brown the chicken on both sides, about 20 minutes. Set chicken on paper towels to drain. Brown the zucchini in another tablespoon or so of oil and drain on paper towels.
4. Lightly spray a 12 × 8-inch baking dish with cooking oil, then place the zucchini into it, overlapping the layers. Top with slices of tomatoes, drizzle with a little oil, then sprinkle with fresh basil leaves. Sprinkle about half of both cheeses over all, then place the chicken on top. Cover the baking dish with a lid or aluminum foil.
5. Bake in the preheated oven for 20 minutes, uncover, sprinkle the remaining cheeses on top, turn the oven up to 425°F, and bake until the cheese is bubbly and brown, about 15 minutes.

Per Serving: 444 calories; 39 g. protein; 23 g. carbohydrate; 22 g. fat; 495 mg. sodium; 152 mg. cholesterol.

Chapter 6

POACHED, ROASTED, BAKED, AND STEAMED CHICKEN

Plain Poached Chicken
Micro-Poached Chicken
Poached Chicken with Ginger Scallion Sauce
Spicy Poached Chicken in Coconut Milk
Poached Chicken Thighs in Chili and Star Anise
Chicken Guadalupe
Spanish-American Chicken
Chicken and Dumplings
Pollo Ensenada
Persian Chicken
Homemade Shake and Bake
Roast Chicken with Fresh Herbs
Chicken Paprikash
Honey Mustard Chicken
Oven-Fried Honey Pecan Chicken

HOW TO POACH A CHICKEN

Although grandmothers might tell you to boil a chicken all day long, it really is not necessary with today's broiler-fryer chickens, which are usually no more than forty-five days old and quite tender to begin with. Besides cooking the bird, the main thing you want to do is to infuse the meat with flavor. One of the best ways to do that is to poach chicken in aromatic broth instead of water.

You can poach a whole chicken or chicken parts on the top of the stove or in the microwave with equally good results. The main thing to remember is that you don't want to let the liquid actually boil, just simmer, and you don't want to overcook white meat or it will become dry and stringy.

Once you have completed the cooking process, cover and let the meat cool down in the aromatic liquid, then lift the meat from the broth, strain the broth, and freeze it for later use in soups and sauces. The chicken meat should be used immediately or covered and refrigerated for up to three days before using.

Plain Poached Chicken

makes 1 pound cooked meat
1¹/₂ hours

1   whole (3 to 4 pound) chicken
1   stalk celery, with leaves
1   carrot, broken into pieces
1   onion, quartered
     Handful of fresh herbs
1   quart chicken broth (see page 24)

1. Place the chicken in a saucepan that just holds it. Cover with vegetables and broth and raise to a simmer.
2. Cook at just under the boil until the bird is tender and the leg joint moves freely, about 1 hour.
3. Cover and cool to room temperature before skinning and boning. Strain broth and freeze.

Micro-Poached Chicken

makes 1 pound cooked meat
30 minutes

1   whole (3 to 4 pound) chicken *or* 6 (4 ounce)
     chicken breasts
2   stalks celery
2   small carrots, broken into pieces
1   medium onion, quartered
     Handful of fresh parsley
³/₄   cup chicken broth

1. Place chicken in a microwaveable casserole. If using chicken pieces arrange them with the meaty parts toward the outside of the dish. Add vegetables and broth. Cover.
2. Microwave at 100 percent (full) power for 22 minutes, then let the chicken stand for 5 minutes before removing it from the oven.

Per ¹/₂ cup serving, mixed light and dark meat: 125 calories; 19 g. protein; 0 g. carbohydrate; 5 g. fat; 49 mg. sodium; 58 mg. cholesterol.

Experiment and you will get interesting taste variations.

- Use apple juice, dry white wine, or beer instead of broth as the poaching liquid;
- add a handful of fresh herbs: tarragon, parsley, oregano, sage, rosemary or thyme;
- throw in some mushrooms, either fresh or dried shiitakes, cepes, boletus, or brown;
- poach giblets in reserved broth and use as an impromptu giblet gravy;
- stir dissolved gelatin into reserved broth (1 package gelatin per 2 cups of broth) and you can make a chicken *en gelée* simply by adding some cooked chicken, pimiento, olives, or celery to the broth. Chill and serve in slices with a dollop of plain yogurt.

Poached Chicken with Ginger Scallion Sauce

Prepare this chicken at your convenience during the day, then leave it to marinate, covered, in the refrigerator until dinner time. Serve over brown rice or butter lettuce.

serves 2
30 minutes

2	**(4 ounce) boneless, skinless chicken breasts**
1	**tablespoon peanut oil**
6	**scallions, green and white parts, thinly sliced on the diagonal**
1/3	**cup fresh ginger, grated**
3	**tablespoons low-sodium soy sauce**
1½	**tablespoons dry sherry**
3	**tablespoons sugar**

1. Place chicken breasts in a medium saucepan and cover with water. Raise to a boil. Simmer until done, about 20 minutes. Cover, and cool in the water.
2. Drain chicken and freeze broth for later use. Tear the chicken into bite-sized pieces, using two forks. Arrange on a flat dish.
3. In an 8-inch skillet, sauté scallions and grated ginger in the oil for about 30 seconds, lift from the skillet, and sprinkle on the chicken.
4. To the same skillet add soy sauce, sherry, and sugar. Boil briefly, then pour over the chicken. Cover and marinate at room temperature about 20 minutes.
5. Serve over butter lettuce or brown rice. This is delicious with curried fruit.

Per Serving: 316 calories; 27 g. protein; 43 g. carbohydrate; 4 g. fat; 1005 mg. sodium; 73 mg. cholesterol.

Spicy Poached Chicken in Coconut Milk

Use seasonings from India, and buy a can of coconut milk from the grocery store, and you've got the makings of a heavenly soup that can begin a multi-course dinner, or stand alone for a family supper that is ready in the time it takes to cook a pot of rice.

serves 4
30 minutes

1	cup basmati or other long grained white rice
2	cups barely salted water
3	tablespoons canola (or other vegetable) oil
1	large yellow onion, finely chopped
4	cloves garlic, minced
1	tablespoon grated fresh ginger
1	dried red chile, crumbled
	Pinch turmeric
1	tablespoon whole coriander seed
2	(4 ounce) boneless, skinless chicken breasts, julienned
1	(14 ounce) can coconut milk
1	cup water
¼	cup fresh cilantro leaves
	Salt to taste
	Cayenne pepper to taste

1. Cook rice, covered, in barely boiling water until tender and all water is absorbed, about 20 minutes. Stir to fluff.

2. While rice is cooking, heat oil over medium heat in the bottom of a medium stockpot. Add onions, frying until golden, stirring frequently, about 10 minutes. Add garlic, ginger, and red chilis, and cook 2 more minutes, stirring constantly. Add turmeric and coriander, stir a moment, then pour in coconut milk and water. Reduce heat to low and cook, uncovered, until the soup thickens, about 10 minutes. Add chicken and simmer, covered, until chicken is opaque, white, and thoroughly cooked, about 5 minutes.

3. Toss in cilantro leaves, season to taste with salt and pepper, and serve over fluffy white rice in wide-rimmed soup bowls.

Per Serving: 571 calories; 27 g. protein; 30 g. carbohydrate; 14 g. fat; 105 mg. sodium; 73 mg. cholesterol.

Poached Chicken Thighs in Chili and Star Anise

Simmering boneless, skinless thigh meat in water perfumed with chili and star anise provides the basis for this main dish. Serve it over butter lettuce with cilantro, crisp red bell pepper strips, scallions, and peanuts and drizzle with rice wine vinaigrette.

serves 4
30 minutes

4   (5 ounce) boneless, skinless chicken thighs
2   cups chicken broth
2   cups cold, fresh tap water
¼   cup chili powder
2   whole star anise

1   tablespoon dried oregano leaves
2   tablespoons brown sugar
1   head butter lettuce, washed and spun dry
¼   cup fresh cilantro leaves
1   red bell pepper, cut into thin strips
6   scallions, finely sliced on the diagonal
¼   cup unsalted roasted peanuts, crushed
2   tablespoons peanut oil
2   tablespoons rice wine vinegar
      Salt to taste
      Freshly ground black pepper to taste

1. Combine chicken thighs, broth, and water in a medium saucepan. Add chili powder, star anise, oregano, and brown sugar. Raise to a simmer and cook, uncovered, until meat is no longer pink in the center, about 20 minutes. Drain, reserving 2 cups liquid.

2. Meanwhile, prepare greens by washing and drying lettuce, separating cilantro leaves from stems, cutting peppers and scallions, and crushing peanuts. (It's easy to crush peanuts in a ziplock bag. Hit them with a mallet or rolling pin.)

3. When the chicken has finished poaching, tear it into shreds using two forks. Boil down 2 cups of the remaining broth over high heat until it is only ⅓ cup.

4. Make the vinaigrette by combining the reduced broth, oil, and vinegar. Season to taste with salt and pepper.

5. To serve, arrange butter lettuce on dinner plates, then compose chicken shreds, red pepper strips, scallions, cilantro leaves, and crushed peanuts on top. Drizzle with vinaigrette and serve.

Per Serving: 293 calories; 32 g. protein; 43 g. carbohydrate; 19 g. fat; 525 mg. sodium; 77 mg. cholesterol.

Chicken Guadalupe

Roast chicken under a glistening coating of honey looks like a movie prop, it's so gorgeous. Skin the bird at the table if you must, but I dare you to keep from sneaking a taste of that crisp, mahogany-colored skin.

serves 4
1 hour

1 **(3 to 4 pound) chicken**
   Zest and juice of 1 lemon
   Salt to taste
   Freshly ground black pepper to taste
   Honey

1. Preheat oven to 400°F.

2. Squeeze lemon juice over the chicken, inside and out, then sprinkle with lemon zest, salt, and pepper. Lay the chicken, breast side up, on an oiled rack over an open roaster and drizzle honey over the visible skin surfaces.

3. Roast in preheated oven until golden brown and thoroughly cooked, about 60 minutes. A meat thermometer inserted into the thickest part should read 180°F. Remove from the oven immediately.

Per Serving: 172 calories; 27 g. protein; 8 g. carbohydrate; 3 g. fat; 65 mg. sodium; 73 mg. cholesterol.

Spanish-American Chicken

Here's a simple supper low in fat and cholesterol but high in satisfaction. Fluffy white rice, green beans, and sliced red tomatoes complete the dinner.

serves 4
1 hour

¹/₂	teaspoon olive oil
4	(4 ounce) boneless, skinless chicken thighs
¹/₂	cup reduced calorie mayonnaise
2	tablespoons white wine vinegar
1	tablespoon chili powder
1	teaspoon oregano leaves
	Salt to taste
	Pepper to taste
¹/₄	cup dry vermouth *or* other white wine
3	scallions, green and white parts, finely sliced
12	large, stuffed green olives, sliced

1. Preheat oven to 375°F.

2. Lightly oil a 12 × 8-inch baking dish with olive oil then arrange chicken pieces, one layer deep in the dish, serve side down. Add wine. Bake, covered, for 20 minutes.

3. Meanwhile, make salad dressing by blending vinegar and seasonings in a bowl. Then, turn the chicken serve side up and brush with the salad dressing mixture.

4. Put oven on broil and broil chicken 7 to 9 inches from heat source for about 10 minutes or until the chicken is fork tender and beginning to brown. Sprinkle with scallions and olives before serving.

Per Serving: 310 calories; 37 g. protein; 51 g. carbohydrate; 6 g. fat; 506 mg. sodium; 114 mg. cholesterol.

Chicken and Dumplings

After you have poached the chicken, simmer the dumplings in the broth for this traditional winter dinner. Remember not to let the cooking water come to a full boil or the dumplings will disintegrate.

serves 4
30 minutes

½	**cup water**
3	**tablespoons margarine**
½	**cup flour**
½	**teaspoon salt**
	Grating of fresh pepper
	Paprika to taste
2	**large eggs**
1	**cup mashed potatoes**
¼	**cup grated Parmesan cheese**
¼	**cup minced fresh parsley**
1	**quart defatted chicken stock (see page 24)**

1. In a medium saucepan, combine water and margarine. Bring to a boil. Season flour with the salt, pepper, and paprika. Lift boiling water off heat then add flour mixture and stir vigorously with a wooden spoon until smooth. Place on heat and cook and stir until the mixture cleans the pan, forms a ball, then leaves a film on the bottom of the pan.

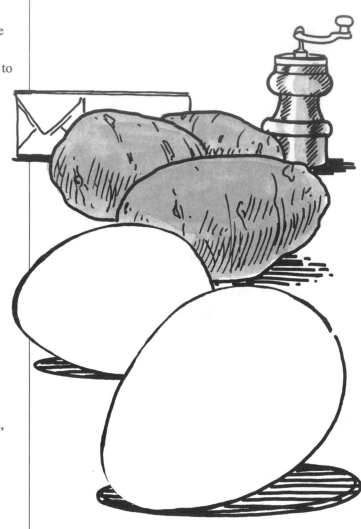

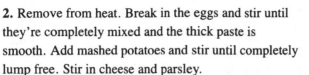

2. Remove from heat. Break in the eggs and stir until they're completely mixed and the thick paste is smooth. Add mashed potatoes and stir until completely lump free. Stir in cheese and parsley.

3. Place chicken broth in a 12-inch skillet and heat just to the simmer. Form dumplings using two teaspoons, then roll each ball in a light dusting of flour. Slip the dumplings into the simmering broth and cook until done, 15 to 20 minutes. They'll sink at first, then, as they cook, they'll float to the top.

4. To serve, place a piece of poached chicken in the bottom of a soup bowl, ladle in some broth, and top with several cooked dumplings. Dust with paprika and serve at once.

Per Serving: 365 calories; 22 g. protein; 26 g. carbohydrate; 18 g. fat; 600 mg. sodium; 103 mg. cholesterol.

Pollo Ensenada

For those who swear that fat will never touch their lips, or hips, again, here's a brightly flavored entree with only 5 grams of fat.

serves 2
30 minutes

2	**(4 ounce) boneless, skinless chicken breasts, poached**
2	**California navel oranges, peeled and sliced into thick rounds**
2	**bright red tomatoes, sliced into thick rounds**
1	**cup peeled and julienned jicama**
1	**red, yellow or green bell pepper, seeded and julienned**
	Sprigs of mint
	Sprigs of cilantro
	Juice of 2 limes
½	**teaspoon chili powder**
	Salt to taste

1. Arrange everything except lime juice, chili powder, and salt on a lettuce-lined platter.

2. Combine lime juice, chili powder and salt, then sprinkle over chicken.

Per Serving: 333 calories; 27 g. protein; 49 g. carbohydrate; 5 g. fat; 89 mg. sodium; 73 mg. cholesterol.

Persian Chicken

Using a steamer, one little fire will cook a lot of food. If you don't have a steamer, rig one by placing a folding steamer basket in the bottom of a big soup pot, then the dish of chicken and fruit in a casserole dish over that.

Rub the bird with spices, then steam it with fruit. The flavors will be mouth-watering, the chicken tender, and the fat and cholesterol load respectable.

serves 4
approximately 2 hours

2	large tart apples, cored and grated
1/2	cup fresh orange juice
1	(3 to 4 pound) chicken, cut into serving pieces
1	teaspoon ground cinnamon
1/2	teaspoon ground cardamom
	Salt to taste
	Freshly ground black pepper to taste
1	large yellow onion, peeled and coarsely chopped
1/4	cup fresh cilantro leaves
1	cup dried fruits: golden raisins, prunes, apricot halves, pears, and currants
1	tablespoon honey

1. Strew grated apple onto the bottom of a large casserole dish that will fit inside the steamer. Pour juice over the apple.

2. Remove and discard fat from the chicken. Rub chicken pieces with cinnamon, cardamom, salt, and pepper. Place chicken over the apple then add onion, cilantro, and dried fruits. Drizzle with honey.

3. Steam until the chicken is tender and the juices run clear, about 2 hours. Serve on a bed of couscous or bulghur.

Per Serving: 438 calories; 38 g. protein; 55 g. carbohydrate; 9 g. fat; 261 mg. sodium; 116 mg. cholesterol.

You can microwave this dish. Arrange food on a 12 × 7-inch microwave baking dish as directed above. Lay the chicken in the dish skin side down, the meaty parts toward the outside of the dish. Cover with clear plastic wrap, taking care that the plastic doesn't touch the meat, then place it in the microwave. Microwave on 100 percent (full) power for 12 minutes, then turn the chicken pieces over and cook 12 more minutes at 100 percent (full) power. Let stand 5 minutes before serving.

Homemade Shake and Bake

For low-fat, oven-fried chicken that is free of additives and good and cheap besides, make up your own homemade seasoning packet.

serves 4
1 hour

4	thigh-leg combination chicken pieces, skinned
½	teaspoon salt
⅛	teaspoon *each:* black pepper, white pepper, and cayenne pepper
¼	teaspoon paprika
3	slices day-old French bread, torn into pieces
2	tablespoons fresh parsley *or* 1 tablespoon dried
2	tablespoons white cornmeal
2	tablespoons walnuts
3	large cloves garlic
1½	teaspoons dry mixed Italian herbs
1	egg white
1	tablespoon water
2	tablespoons Dijon mustard
1	teaspoon honey

1. Preheat the oven to 400°F.

2. Place chicken pieces on a piece of waxed paper and sprinkle with ¼ teaspoon salt, the peppers, and paprika. Set aside.

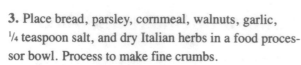

3. Place bread, parsley, cornmeal, walnuts, garlic, ¼ teaspoon salt, and dry Italian herbs in a food processor bowl. Process to make fine crumbs.

4. Whisk egg white with water, mustard, and honey and dip chicken pieces in to thoroughly coat. Press crumb mixture over the chicken pieces and arrange on a lightly greased rack.

5. Bake in preheated oven on the rack over a cookie sheet until crisp, brown, fork tender, and the juices run clear, about 40 minutes.

Per Serving: 308 calories; 26 g. protein; 9 g. carbohydrate; 4 g. fat; 254 mg. sodium; 82 mg. cholesterol.

Roast Chicken with Fresh Herbs

Nothing could be simpler than roasting a chicken. Lift the skin over the breast and place fresh herbs between skin and meat, and you have a dinner fit for company. A golden brown bird with crisp skin, moist meat, and very little fat. Have some left over? Use it for Cranberry Chicken Salad (see pp. 22).

serves 4
1¼ hours

1 **(3 to 4 pound) chicken**
   Salt to taste
   Black pepper to taste
   Red pepper to taste
   White pepper to taste
   Fresh herbs

1. Preheat the oven to 400°F.

2. Pull any loose fat from the cavity of the bird and discard. Rub the bird inside and out with salt and peppers. Lift the skin over the breast with your fingers and arrange fresh herbs (sage, parsley, tarragon, thyme, and/or oregano) under the skin. Tie the legs together, then tie them to the tail with cotton string.

3. Place the chicken on an oiled rack in the middle of the oven so that hot air can flow freely around the bird. Place a pan to catch dripping fat on the lower shelf of the oven.

4. Roast in the preheated oven until juices run clear when the flesh is pierced, and the drumstick moves freely when lifted, about 1 hour. A meat thermometer inserted in the thickest part of the breast should read 180°F.

Per Serving: 140 calories; 27 g. protein; 0 g. carbohydrate; 3 g. fat; 64 mg. sodium; 73 mg. cholesterol.

Chicken Paprikash

The traditional Hungarian recipe calls for sour cream, but you can lighten this dish considerably by using plain nonfat yogurt instead. A cup of sour cream has 495 calories and 102 milligrams of cholesterol, but the same amount of nonfat plain yogurt has only 125 calories and 4 milligrams of cholesterol. The difference in taste is minimal.

Cook noodles and stir in green peas just before serving to complete.

serves 4
1 hour

1	tablespoon Hungarian paprika
1½	pounds boneless, skinless chicken thighs
4	tablespoons olive oil
2	tablespoons finely chopped onions
1	cup finely sliced brown mushrooms
1	(8 ounce) carton plain nonfat yogurt
½	cup dry white wine
	Salt to taste
	Pepper to taste

1. Rub paprika into the flesh of the chicken and set aside.

2. In a 10-inch skillet, heat olive oil over medium-high heat then brown onions and mushrooms. Remove vegetables from the skillet, then add chicken and brown on all sides.

3. Add vegetables to skillet with chicken. Mix the yogurt and white wine together and pour over the chicken. Cover and simmer until chicken is fork tender, about 45 minutes. Season to taste with salt and pepper.

Per Serving: 311 calories; 22 g. protein; 8 g. carbohydrate; 19 g. fat; 95 mg. sodium; 59 mg. cholesterol.

Honey Mustard Chicken

An all-American favorite, this popular supper entree is quick and easy to prepare. Serve with rice or mashed potatoes, a green salad, and you're set.

serves 4
45 minutes

¼ cup ball park–style yellow mustard
3 tablespoons honey
Juice and zest of half a lemon
⅔ cup plain bread crumbs
1 pound boneless, skinless chicken thighs
Salt to taste
Pepper to taste
1 tablespoon canola (or other vegetable) oil

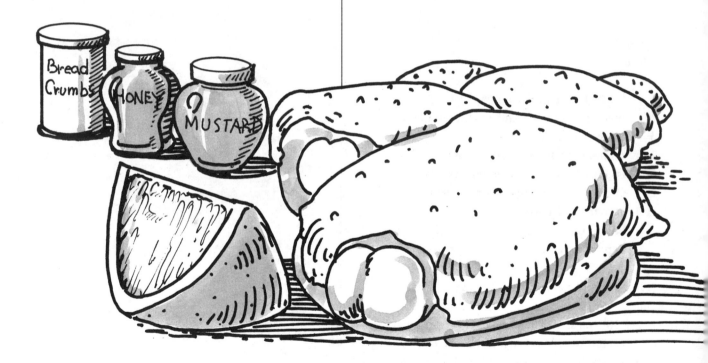

1. Preheat the oven to 375°F.

2. Prepare a glass utility dish just big enough to hold the meat with nonstick spray.

3. Combine mustard, honey, and lemon juice in a small bowl. Place bread crumbs on a piece of wax paper. Dip chicken pieces first into honey mustard then in bread crumbs. Season to taste with salt and pepper. Place in the glass dish, and do not allow the sides to touch. Drizzle evenly with oil.

4. Bake, uncovered, in preheated oven until golden brown and cooked through, about 30 to 35 minutes.

Per Serving: 298 calories; 24 g. protein; 28 g. carbohydrate; 10 g. fat; 672 mg. sodium; 95 mg. cholesterol.

To make bread crumbs, toss leftover bread into a food processor or blender and whirl into crumbs. Store in a small jar in the freezer and you'll always have them on hand. If you want to make Italian-flavored crumbs, just throw in a little parsley, some dried Italian herbs, and a spoonful of grated parmesan.

Oven-Fried Honey Pecan Chicken

Crunchy, spicy chicken pieces of your choice, cooked no-fat in the oven, make ideal picnic fare. These are delicious hot or at room temperature.

serves 8 to 10
1 hour

18	chicken pieces of your choice, skinned
2	cups pecans
1/2	cup unbleached white flour
1	cup yellow cornmeal
1	tablespoon paprika
2	teaspoons cayenne pepper
1/4	teaspoon white pepper
1/2	teaspoon finely milled black pepper
2	teaspoons salt
2	large eggs
1/2	cup plain nonfat yogurt
2	tablespoons mild honey

Dipping Sauce

1/4	cup (1/2 stick) butter
1/4	cup honey

1. Preheat the oven to 375°F.

2. Remove skin and fat from chicken pieces, then wash and dry with a paper towel.

3. Finely chop pecans in a food processor or blender, then combine with flour, cornmeal, paprika, peppers, and salt. Mix in a pie plate.

4. In a large bowl, whisk together the eggs, yogurt, and honey. Dip chicken pieces into this mixture, then in the pecan mixture. Coat pieces on all sides then lay on an ovenproof rack.

5. Bake on a rake placed over a cookie sheet in the preheated oven until crisp and cooked through, about 30 minutes.

6. To make dipping sauce, stir ingredients together. Serve in a small bowl to accompany the chicken.

7. Serve hot or at room temperature with dipping sauce.

Per Serving: 320 calories; 31 g. protein; 12 g. carbohydrate; 9 g. fat; 194 mg. sodium; 87 mg. cholesterol.

Chapter 7

COMPANY'S COMING

Diana's Roast Chicken in a Nest
Lemon Zest Chicken
Larry Elder's Chicken Medallions and Grits
Braised Chicken with Artichoke Hearts and
Brown Mushrooms
Out-of-this-World Chicken
Connie Emerson's Tunisian Mint Chicken
Mama's Buttermilk-Fried Chicken
Grilled Chicken Breast on Mesclun with
Fresh Herbs
Chicken with Forty Cloves of Garlic
Tuscany Chicken
Clara Platt's Apricot-Glazed Chicken
Coq au Vin
Morel-stuffed Chicken Breasts
Roast Chicken with Root Vegetables
Chicken Dijon in Tarragon and
Dry Vermouth

Diana's Roast Chicken in a Nest

Diana serves this colorful roast chicken nestled in a bed of braised lettuce and grated carrot on a peach-colored platter garnished with small, icy-cold pickled beets. The golden bird, the bright green lettuce nest flecked with orange shards then garnished with ruby-red beets—it's almost too beautiful to eat. You can also make this with game hens, roasting them about an hour.

serves 4
1¹/₂ hours

1	(3 to 4 pound) roasting chicken
1	bunch cilantro
6	sage leaves
	Salt to taste
	Freshly ground black pepper to taste
1	cup dry white wine
1	head iceberg lettuce, sliced vertically into 6 pieces
1	large carrot, scraped and shredded
¹/₂	teaspoon cornstarch
1	tablespoon European-style Dijon stone-ground mustard with whole seeds
2	tablespoons butter
4	tablespoons half and half
	Small whole red pickled beets (garnish)

1. Preheat the oven to 400°F.

2. Remove and discard all excess fat from the cavity of the chicken, then wash and pat the bird dry.

3. Stuff the cavity with cilantro leaves. Lift the skin over the breast meat with your fingers and arrange sage leaves under the skin in an attractive pattern. Tie legs and tail together. Season to taste with salt and pepper. Place on an oiled rack over a roasting pan.

4. Roast the chicken until skin is crisp golden brown and the juices will run clear, about 1 hour 15 minutes. A thermometer inserted into the thickest part of the meat should read 180°F.

5. Place chicken on a platter. Remove and discard the cilantro in the cavity. Degrease the roasting pan then place on top of the stove and raise the pan juices to a boil. Scrape up the browned bits clinging to the pan, add wine a little at a time, and continue to scrape. Bring the liquid to a boil. Drop lettuce and carrots into the boiling pan juices, cover, and braise 4 minutes. Lift the vegetables from boiling juice to a colander to drain, then arrange under and around the chicken on the platter. Hold in a warm oven while you make the sauce.

6. Boiling on high, reduce pan juices by half, then stir in cornstarch that has been made into a paste with a little cold water. Cook and stir the sauce until thick. Swirl in mustard, butter and half and half. Season to taste with salt and pepper. Pour the sauce over the chicken.

7. Nestle groups of cold baby pickled beets on the lettuce, decorate with additional sage leaves, and serve immediately.

Per Serving: 391 calories; 29 g. protein; 8 g. carbohydrate; 19 g. fat; 300 mg. sodium; 120 mg. cholesterol.

Lemon Zest Chicken

Terrific for lunch served in puff pastry shells, you can also offer this crunchy melange on a bed of butter lettuce. If you're using puff pastry, bake the shells while you're preparing the rest of the dish and you'll save time.

serves 6
1 hour

2	**(4 ounce) boneless, skinless chicken breasts**
4	**hard-boiled eggs, chopped**
2	**cups chopped celery**
½	**cup water chestnuts**
1	**cup almonds**
1	**teaspoon butter**

Dressing

1	**tablespoon minced onion**
1	**cup reduced-calorie mayonnaise**
	Juice and zest of half a lemon
1	**cup grated low-fat cheddar cheese**
4	**puff pastry shells, cooked according to package directions**

1. Preheat the oven to 400°F.

2. Butter a 2-quart casserole dish.

3. Micropoach chicken breasts by cooking with ½ cup water or broth in a microwave dish covered with plastic wrap that doesn't touch the meat. Microwave at 100 percent (full) power for 8 minutes. Let chicken stand 5 minutes, then cut into bite-size pieces.

4. In a medium bowl, combine the cooked chicken, chopped eggs, celery, and water chestnuts. Toss lightly and set aside.

5. In a small skillet, brown the almonds in butter then remove from heat and chop finely. Add to chicken mixture and toss.

6. To make the dressing, combine the minced onion, mayonnaise, and lemon juice and zest in a small bowl then toss with chicken.

7. Place mixture in prepared dish, top with grated cheese, and bake, uncovered, 20 minutes. Serve in puff pastry shells garnished with a lemon twist.

Per Serving: 422 calories; 20 g. protein; 9 g. carbohydrate; 27 g. fat; 451 mg. sodium; 65 mg. cholesterol.

• To reduce calories and fat, substitute plain yogurt for half the mayonnaise and reduce the cheese by half.

Larry Elder's Chicken Medallions and Grits

National Chicken Cooking Contest Winner, North Carolina, 1991

A heavenly fusion of Southern and Southwestern cooking, this dish is glamorous to serve. It's lovely with a quick salad of green pepper, orange slices, and red onion rings drizzled with olive oil. Don't forget the corn bread.

serves 4
1 hour

4	(4 ounce) boneless, skinless chicken breasts
1	teaspoon ground cumin
4	cups water
½	teaspoon salt
1	cup quick-cooking grits
2	tablespoons butter

Southern Salsa

1	cup whole kernel corn, cooked and drained
1	cup cooked black-eyed peas, rinsed and drained
1	medium tomato, chopped
1	small cucumber, peeled, seeded, and diced
¼	cup diced scallions, green and white parts
2	tablespoons fresh lemon juice
2	tablespoons minced fresh basil leaves
1	small fresh jalapeño pepper, seeded and minced
1	clove garlic, minced
	Salt to taste
	Pepper to taste

1. Flatten chicken breasts between waxed paper to ½ inch thickness. Rub cumin into chicken breasts and set aside.

2. In a medium saucepan, combine water and salt and raise to a boil. Stir in grits and cook according to package directions. Spoon cooked grits into a greased 9-inch square baking pan, cover, and refrigerate until firm.

3. Heat butter in a 10-inch skillet over medium heat, then cook chicken, turning, until fork tender and brown, about 12 minutes.

4. While chicken is cooking make the salsa by combining all ingredients in a large bowl. Cover and reserve.

5. Once chicken is cooked remove it from the skillet and drain on paper towels. Cover and keep warm.

6. Invert the baking pan to remove the grits, then cut into 4 squares. Cut each square into 2 triangles. Add grits to the skillet and cook, turning once, until crisp and lightly brown.

7. To serve, cut each chicken breast half crosswise against the grain to form medallions. Place medallions from 1 breast on each serving plate with 2 grits cakes. Spoon salsa over cakes.

Per Serving: 330 calories; 32 g. protein; 28 g. carbohydrate; 9 g. fat; 130 mg. sodium; 89 mg. cholesterol.

Braised Chicken with Artichoke Hearts and Brown Mushrooms

Here's a recipe that's survived from the fifties, now made by the sons and daughters of cooks who thought they'd arrived when they discovered canned artichoke hearts. You can double this recipe easily to feed a larger group.

serves 4
1½ hours

4	**(4 ounce) boneless, skinless chicken breasts**
	Salt to taste
	Pepper to taste
	Paprika to taste
2	**tablespoons butter or margarine**
1	**cup artichoke hearts, drained**
½	**pound brown mushrooms, thinly sliced**
6	**scallions, green and white parts, thinly sliced**
2	**tablespoons unbleached white flour**
½	**cup chicken broth**
½	**cup dry sherry**
¼	**teaspoon rosemary needles**

1. Rub chicken breasts with salt, pepper, and paprika.

2. Place butter in a large skillet, brown chicken pieces until golden, about 10 minutes, then transfer to a large casserole dish. Arrange artichoke hearts among the chicken pieces.

3. Sauté the mushrooms and scallions in the remaining butter until tender and golden, about 5 minutes. Sprinkle flour over the vegetables and cook a few moments. Stir in broth, sherry, and rosemary. Cook and stir until sauce thickens.

4. Pour sauce over the chicken, cover, and bake at 375°F until chicken is tender, about 30 minutes.

Per Serving: 264 calories; 29 g. protein; 12 g. carbohydrate; 15 g. fat; 442 mg. sodium; 105 mg. cholesterol.

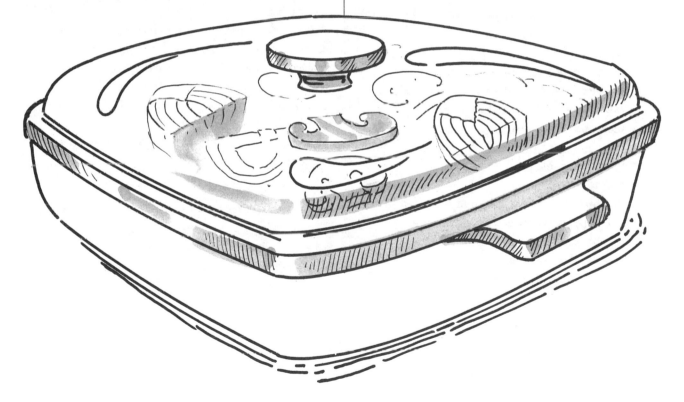

Out-of-this-World Chicken

Here's a one-pot dinner that makes its own gravy, looks inviting served on a platter of rice, and is good for you. Don't be daunted by the long list of ingredients; it goes together quickly.

serves 8
2 hours

4	tablespoons butter or margarine
8	small pearl onions, peeled
8	shallots, peeled
4	cloves garlic, minced
8	(4 ounce) boneless, skinless chicken breasts
2	tablespoons unbleached white flour
½	teaspoon curry powder
½	teaspoon fresh thyme leaves *or* a pinch dried
1	teaspoon whole peppercorns
	Salt to taste
4	medium carrots, scraped and julienned
1	bell pepper, yellow or red, seeded and julienned
1	cup small mushrooms
¼	cup finely cut fresh parsley
1	cup dry red wine
1	cup chicken broth
3	medium tomatoes, minced
½	cup golden raisins
½	cup toasted slivered almonds

1. Heat 2 tablespoons butter in a 10-inch skillet until foamy. Add pearl onions, shallots, and garlic. Sauté until golden, about 10 minutes, then remove the vegetables and place in the bottom of a large glass baking dish.

2. Rub chicken breasts with a mixture of flour, curry powder, and thyme leaves. Brown in the remaining 2 tablespoons butter with peppercorns until breasts are golden brown on both sides, about 10 minutes. Remove the chicken from the skillet and place in a baking dish.

3. Add carrots, pepper, mushrooms, and parsley to the chicken, then pour wine and broth over. Top with minced tomatoes. Cover and bake in 350°F oven until tender, about 1½ hours. During the last 15 minutes, remove the lid, add raisins and almonds, salt to taste, and finish baking, uncovered.

4. Serve on a platter of rice, using the pan juices as a sauce served on the side.

Per Serving: 306 calories; 30 g. protein; 18 g. carbohydrate; 12 g. fat; 240 mg. sodium; 88 mg. cholesterol.

Connie Emerson's Tunisian Mint Chicken

National Chicken Cooking Contest Winner, Nevada, 1991

This Middle Eastern dish goes best with couscous.

serves 4
45 minutes

½   cup unbleached white flour
1   tablespoon lemon pepper
1   (3 pound) chicken, cut into serving pieces
3   tablespoons olive oil

Sauce

6   fresh mint leaves
¼   cup diced green bell pepper
½   teaspoon coriander
¼   cup diced yellow onion
3   medium tomatoes, diced

1. Combine flour and lemon pepper in a shallow bowl and dredge chicken pieces to coat. Set aside.
2. Heat oil in a 10-inch skillet over medium-high heat. Cook chicken, turning, until fork tender and golden brown on all sides, about 35 minutes.
3. While the chicken is cooking, combine sauce ingredients in a small saucepan and cook over moderate heat, stirring, about 15 minutes. Reserve.
4. To serve, place chicken pieces on a bed of couscous and top with sauce.

Per Serving: 245 calories; 32 g. protein; 4 g. carbohydrate; 9 g. fat; 269 mg. sodium; 87 mg. cholesterol.

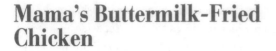

Mama's Buttermilk-Fried Chicken

Old-fashioned, crusty fried chicken is practically a lost art, and once in a while, there's nothing like fried chicken, mashed potatoes, sop gravy, and green beans for dinner. Oh . . . don't forget to pass the biscuits.

I always fry chicken in my mama's black skillet, and I use a deep fat thermometer to hold the temperature of the oil to 350°F.

If you're a real purist, soak the chicken overnight in the buttermilk. For me, that's one step too many. I feel martyred enough by the fat-splashed stove without trying to rearrange the refrigerator to hold chicken the day before.

serves 8
1 hour

2	**fryers, cut into serving pieces**
2	**cups unbleached white flour**
1½	**teaspoons baking powder**
1½	**teaspoons baking soda**
½	**teaspoon salt**
¼	**teaspoon *each:* black pepper, white pepper, and cayenne pepper**
3	**cups buttermilk**
	Canola oil for deep frying

1. Wash and dry chicken pieces.

2. Place flour in a paper sack, then, two pieces at a time, twist the sack closed and shake chicken pieces in the flour to coat. Remove pieces and shake any excess flour back into the sack.

3. Mix baking powder, baking soda, salt, and peppers into the flour.

4. Pour buttermilk into a deep bowl. Dip each chicken piece into buttermilk then back into the flour mixture in the sack. Shake well so that each piece is completely flour coated.

5. After all pieces are ready to fry, heat oil in a large, deep skillet to a temperature of 350°F. Fry chicken a few pieces at a time until golden brown all over, turning from time to time. Transfer chicken pieces to an ovenproof platter and finish cooking in a 350°F oven for 15 to 20 minutes. Serve piping hot.

Per Serving: 365 calories; 35 g. protein; 13 g. carbohydrate; 18 g. fat; 385 mg. sodium; 119 mg. cholesterol.

To make good sop gravy from the drippings, drain all but ¼ cup of the fat from the skillet, leaving all the crispies in the skillet. Add 2 to 3 tablespoons unbleached white flour and make a golden roux, stirring over medium heat. Pour in 1 pint of cold milk. Cook and stir until the gravy is thick. Season to taste with salt, and black, red, and white peppers. Some people add a drop or two of Worcestershire sauce. And don't forget those biscuits.

Grilled Chicken Breast on Mesclun with Fresh Herbs

Mesclun is the name French market gardeners give to the small, odd leaves of greens they package together in a spirit of waste not, want not. You can buy ready-packaged Mesclun in many city markets today, or you can make your own by combining small leaves of oak leaf lettuce, arugula, Belgian endive, red-tipped lettuce, spinach, or any other greens you may find. The idea is to create a bed of tender greens, used here to pillow a grill-marked chicken breast. Add a quartered tomato, sprinkle with a mixture of fresh herbs, and you have dinner that's dazzling to look at, delicious, fresh, and low in calories.

serves 4
45 minutes

4	**(4 ounce) boneless, skinless chicken breasts**
	Salt to taste
	Freshly ground black pepper to taste
¼	**cup olive oil**
4	**cups Mesclun *or* mixed salad greens**
2	**medium tomatoes, quartered**
4	**tablespoons balsamic vinegar**
1	**tablespoon chopped fresh rosemary needles *or* 1 teaspoon dried**
1	**tablespoon fresh oregano leaves *or* 1 teaspoon dried**

1. Flatten breasts between sheets of waxed paper to ¹/₂ inch thickness. Season to taste with salt and pepper. Coat with 1 tablespoon of oil, then cover and refrigerate while the charcoal grill preheats.
2. Divide the mixed greens among four dinner plates. Add tomato wedges to each plate. Combine vinegar and remaining oil in a small saucepan and warm over low heat.
3. Grill chicken breasts over hot coals until cooked through and grill-marked, no more than 2 to 3 minutes per side. Remove to a bowl and toss with fresh herbs, rosemary and oregano. Scoop each cooked breast onto a bed of mesclun on a dinner plate, drizzle warmed vinaigrette over, grate pepper over, then serve immediately.

Per Serving: 190 calories; 27 g. protein; 0 g. carbohydrate; 13 g. fat; 64 mg. sodium; 73 mg. cholesterol.

Chicken with Forty Cloves of Garlic

Even though it sounds like a lot of work to peel forty cloves of garlic, about 2 big heads, the job's made easier if you douse the garlic in boiling water about 30 seconds then whack the cloves under the flat side of a chef's knife. Once the chicken is cooked, grill thick slices of French bread and smear the soft, sweet, roasted garlic on instead of butter. Toss a salad. Make iced tea. It's a summer picnic.

serves 4
1 hour

1	**(3 to 4 pound) chicken cut into serving pieces**
40	**cloves fresh garlic (about 2 large heads)**
¹/₂	**cup dry white wine**
¹/₄	**cup dry vermouth**
¹/₄	**cup olive oil**
1	**tablespoon fresh oregano *or* 1 teaspoon dried**
2	**tablespoons fresh basil leaves *or* 2 teaspoons dried**
6	**sprigs minced parsley**
	Salt to taste
	Cayenne pepper to taste
	Black pepper to taste
	Juice and zest of 1 lemon

1. Preheat oven to 375°F.

2. Place chicken pieces in a shallow glass baking dish, skin side up. Sprinkle all ingredients except the lemon over the chicken. Cut zest from the lemon and sprinkle onto the chicken, then squeeze the juice over the chicken. Cover the pan tightly with lid or aluminum foil.

3. Bake chicken in the preheated oven for 40 minutes. Remove the lid and continue cooking until the chicken skin is a crisp golden brown, the meat is thoroughly done and tender, and the juices run clear, about 15 more minutes.

4. Serve pieces of chicken and roasted garlic alongside thick slices of grilled French bread.

Per Serving: 180 calories; 27 g. protein; 0 g. carbohydrate; 6 g. fat; 64 mg. sodium; 73 mg. cholesterol.

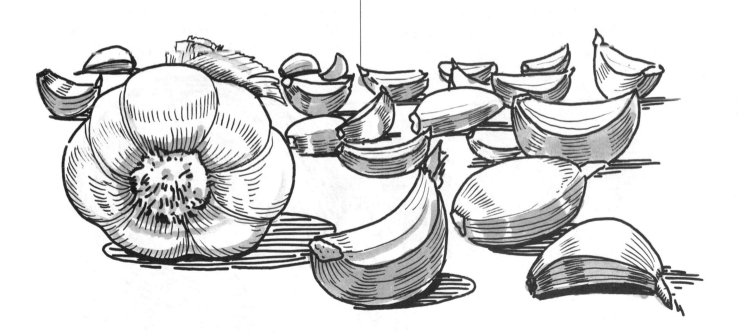

Tuscany Chicken

Accompany this chicken with red pepper-spiked polenta, a salad of mixed greens, a glass of red wine, and a loaf of crusty French bread. Viva Italia via the U.S. of A. Good old American Miracle Whip makes it ours.

serves 4

1 hour

2	tablespoons olive oil
4	(4 ounce) boneless, skinless chicken breasts
¼	cup Miracle Whip salad dressing
6	scallions, green and white parts, sliced into 1-inch pieces
1	green bell pepper, chopped
1	tablespoon tomato paste
2	cloves garlic, minced
	Salt to taste
	Pepper to taste
1	eggplant, peeled and sliced
1	medium tomato, sliced
¼	cup chopped parsley
2	tablespoons fresh basil leaves, bruised *or* 2 teaspoons dried

1. Preheat oven to 375°F.

2. Lightly oil a large baking dish with olive oil.

3. Heat remaining oil in a 10-inch skillet over medium-high heat, then brown chicken breasts on both sides. Remove breasts to baking dish and reserve.

4. Stir the Miracle Whip, scallions, pepper, tomato paste, garlic, salt, and pepper into the skillet. Cook until vegetables are tender, about 10 minutes, then spoon the mixture over the chicken.

5. Arrange eggplant and tomato slices over the chicken. Sprinkle with parsley, basil, and salt and pepper to taste. Cover the dish and bake in the preheated oven until chicken and vegetables are tender, about 25 minutes. Serve with polenta or over rice.

Per Serving: 369 calories; 37 g. protein; 58 g. carbohydrate; 18 g. fat; 251 mg. sodium; 107 mg. cholesterol.

Clara Platt's Apricot-Glazed Chicken

National Chicken Cooking Contest Winner, Wyoming, 1991

The only thing better than the looks of chicken glazed with a rosy orange-apricot sauce is the taste. Clara Platt serves this garnished with endive and apricot halves.

serves 8
1 hour

8	**(4 ounce) boneless, skinless chicken breasts**
2	**teaspoons olive oil**
1	**clove garlic, minced**
¹/₂	**teaspoon lemon pepper**
2	**tablespoons lemon juice**
10	**dried apricots**
³/₄	**cup fresh orange juice**
1	**teaspoon Dijon mustard**
1	**teaspoon brown sugar**
¹/₂	**teaspoon ground ginger**

1. Preheat the oven to 350°F.

2. Place chicken breasts in a flat baking dish. In a small bowl combine the olive oil, garlic, lemon pepper, and lemon juice. Brush onto all surfaces of the chicken and bake in the preheated oven for 30 minutes.

3. While the chicken is cooking, combine apricots and orange juice in a medium saucepan. Raise to a boil, then reduce heat and simmer 15 minutes, or until apricots are tender. Stir in mustard, brown sugar, and ginger. Simmer 2 more minutes then place in a food processor or blender and puree.

4. Coat chicken with apricot sauce and continue to bake until chicken is fork tender and cooked through, about 30 minutes.

5. Run the chicken under the broiler to brown, then place on a serving dish, garnish with endive and apricot halves, and serve immediately.

Per Serving: 272 calories; 31 g. protein; 73 g. carbohydrate; 8 g. fat; 164 mg. sodium; 19 mg. cholesterol.

Coq Au Vin

The taste of chicken cooked with rich red burgundy and mushrooms is hard to match. Brown mushrooms taste better than white button mushrooms, and Porcini taste best of all. Mix two or three kinds of mushrooms if you wish. You can even toss in rehydrated Oriental shiitakes.

serves 4
2 hours

8	(1½ pounds) boneless, skinless chicken thighs
	Flour
	Salt
	Pepper
	Nutmeg
	Paprika
3	slices bacon, diced
4	tablespoons butter or margarine
2	cups tiny pearl onions
1	clove garlic, pressed
1	bay leaf
	Pinch of thyme
1	cup sliced fresh mushrooms
1	cup dry red Burgundy
1	cup chicken broth
	Italian flat-leaf parsley

1. Preheat the oven to 325°F.
2. Dredge chicken thighs in flour seasoned with salt, pepper, nutmeg, and paprika. Set aside.
3. In a roasting pan over medium heat, fry bacon until crisp, then remove. Add butter to roaster, then brown onions, garlic, bay leaf and thyme for a few moments. Add chicken pieces and brown on all sides.
4. Add mushrooms and continue to brown a few minutes.
5. Place cooked bacon in the roaster, pour in wine and broth, cover, and bake in the preheated oven until meat is fork tender, about an hour. Sprinkle with Italian flat leaf parsley before serving.

Per Serving: 426 calories; 34 g. protein; 10 g. carbohydrate; 22 g. fat; 276 mg. sodium; 122 mg. cholesterol.

Morel-Stuffed Chicken Breasts

Morels, genus *Morchella,* are a brownish, sponged, cap mushroom with a distinct conical shape that pop up in springtime. Rare and expensive, the morel has such a distinctive flavor that a small serving will linger in your memory a long time. Year round, dried morels are sold in gourmet shops. Rehydrated, just a small amount offers an intense forest taste that enhances many a dish.

serves 2
1 hour

2	**(4 ounce) boneless, skinless chicken breasts**
½	**cup fresh morels (can substitute other mushrooms), finely chopped**
2	**gorgeous morels for garnish**
1	**tablespoon butter**
1	**large egg**
1	**teaspoon brandy**
1	**tablespoon finely chopped parsley**
	Salt to taste
	Freshly ground black pepper to taste
	Pinch of cayenne pepper
	Pinch of white pepper
2	**tablespoons bread crumbs**
	Red pepper to taste
	Melted butter to coat the baking pan and drizzle atop the rolls
2	**tablespoons dry sherry**

1. Preheat the oven to 350°F.

2. Flatten chicken breasts between sheets of waxed paper to ½ inch thickness.

3. In a small skillet, sauté the chopped and whole mushrooms in butter until most of the liquid evaporates. Reserve whole mushrooms for garnish. Remove chopped mushrooms and place in a small bowl. Combine with butter, egg, brandy, parsley, salt, peppers, and bread crumbs.

4. Divide the mushroom filling between the chicken breasts and roll up, folding like an envelope so that the stuffing does not fall out. Fasten the chicken envelopes shut with toothpicks.

5. Butter a small 6 × 6-inch baking pan. Choose one that can be used on top of the stove as well as in the oven, then place the breasts, seam side down, in the dish. Drizzle with a little more melted butter and dust with black and red pepper.

6. Bake the chicken rolls in the preheated oven, uncovered, until done, about 35 minutes, basting from time to time with butter.

7. Place the chicken on dinner plates then deglaze the pan with the sherry. Pour over the rolls, garnish with reserved sauteed morels, and serve.

Per Serving: 357 calories; 31 g. protein; 9 g. carbohydrate; 17 g. fat; 290 mg. sodium; 241 mg. cholesterol.

Roast Chicken with Root Vegetables

One of the traditional Friday favorites, this American ceremonial dinner has withstood the test of time. It tastes best when made with a kosher roasting chicken, if you can find it.

serves 4
1 hour, plus marinating overnight

1	**(3 to 4 pound) chicken**
1	**cup olive oil**
2	**cloves garlic, pressed**
4	**sprigs fresh thyme *or* ¾ teaspoon dried**
4	**carrots, scraped, cut in half horizontally and vertically**
12	**pearl onions, peeled**
8	**small red roasting potatoes, scrubbed**
2	**teaspoons salt**
1	**teaspoon freshly ground black pepper**
1	**teaspoon Hungarian paprika**
¼	**teaspoon cayenne pepper**

1. Place chicken in a glass dish.
2. Combine oil, garlic, and thyme. Pour ½ cup of this marinade into a covered jar and refrigerate. Rub remaining marinade into chicken, inside and out. Cover chicken and refrigerate overnight, turning from time to time.

3. An hour and a half before serving time, preheat the oven to 450°F.
4. Pour marinade from the covered jar into the bottom of a 10-inch cast-iron skillet or roaster. Add carrots, onions, and potatoes. Stir to coat with marinade. Lift chicken from marinade and discard any remaining liquid in the bottom of the dish. Season generously with salt and peppers and place on top of the vegetables, pulling some up to make a nest around the bird. Season vegetables to taste with salt and pepper.
5. Place the chicken in the preheated oven. After 10 minutes, turn the heat down to 400°F. Roast until juices run clear and leg joint moves freely, about 50 to 55 minutes. A thermometer inserted into the thickest portion should read 180°F. Baste from time to time with marinade in the bottom of the pan. Let stand 5 minutes before serving.

Per Serving: 442 calories; 32 g. protein; 12 g. carbohydrate; 7 g. fat; 206 mg. sodium; 73 mg. cholesterol.

Chicken Dijon in Tarragon and Dry Vermouth

Scandalously easy to prepare, this chicken dish is delicious accompanied by potatoes Anna and French-cut green beans. Feel free to substitute any white wine for the vermouth.

serves 4
1 hour

1½	pounds boneless, skinless chicken breasts and thighs
2	tablespoons Dijon mustard
1	cup dry vermouth
3	tablespoons fresh tarragon *or* 1 tablespoon dried
	Freshly ground black pepper to taste

1. Place chicken in a shallow baking dish small enough so that the chicken pieces fit snugly. Smear mustard over the chicken, then pour on wine. Sprinkle with tarragon and pepper.

2. Cover the dish tightly with a lid or aluminum foil. Bake for 45 minutes in a 350°F oven.

3. Remove the cover and place the chicken under the broiler a minute or so to brown. Serve hot.

Per Serving: 195 calories; 12 g. protein; 8 g. carbohydrate; 3 g. fat; 50 mg. sodium; 90 mg. cholesterol.

NOTES

NOTES

KITCHEN METRICS

For cooking and baking convenience, the Metric Commission of Canada suggests the following for adapting to metric measurement. The table gives approximate, rather than exact, conversions.

SPOONS

¼ teaspoon	= 1	milliliter
½ teaspoon	= 2	milliliters
1 teaspoon	= 5	milliliters
1 tablespoon	= 15	milliliters
2 tablespoons	= 25	milliliters
3 tablespoons	= 50	milliliters

CUPS

¼ cup	= 50	milliliters
⅓ cup	= 75	milliliters
½ cup	= 125	milliliters
⅔ cup	= 150	milliliters
¾ cup	= 175	milliliters
1 cup	= 250	milliliters

OVEN TEMPERATURES

200°F	=	100°C
225°F	=	110°C
250°F	=	120°C
275°F	=	140°C
300°F	=	150°C
325°F	=	160°C
350°F	=	180°C
375°F	=	190°C
400°F	=	200°C
425°F	=	220°C
450°F	=	230°C
475°F	=	240°C

INDEX

ABOUT THE AUTHOR

Linda West Eckhardt is the author of eight cookbooks including *The Only Texas Cookbook, Barbecue Indoors and Out,* and *Bread in Half the Time,* winner of the 1990 International Association of Culinary Professionals Award for Best Cookbook of the Year.

She also writes weekly newspaper columns for *The Oregonian* and for *The Medford Mail Tribune.* In addition, she has published more than 100 magazine articles, a dozen short stories in literary journals, and has fiction included in the anthologies *South by Southwest* and *A Texas Christmas.* She has edited cookbooks and a literary anthology and teaches writing and cooking. Her works in progress include another cookbook and a novel.

Eckhardt lives in Ashland, Oregon with her psychiatrist husband Joe, two dogs and two cats. Between them they have six grown children.